MARVEL

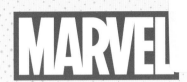

COSPLAY ★ ★ ★ the ★ ★ ★ MARVEL WAY

MARVEL

COSPLAY
the MARVEL WAY

★ ★ ★

A Guide to Costuming Culture and Crafting Basics

JUDY STEPHENS

Running Press
PHILADELPHIA

Running Press
Hachette Book Group
1290 Avenue of the Americas, New York, NY 10104
www.runningpress.com
@Running_Press

Printed in China

First Edition: June 2024

Published by Running Press, an imprint of Hachette Book Group, Inc. The Running Press name and logo are trademarks of Hachette Book Group, Inc.

The Hachette Speakers Bureau provides a wide range of authors for speaking events. To find out more, go to www.hachettespeakersbureau.com or email HachetteSpeakers@hbgusa.com.

Running Press books may be purchased in bulk for business, educational, or promotional use. For more information, please contact your local bookseller or the Hachette Book Group Special Markets Department at Special.Markets@hbgusa.com.

MARVEL PUBLISHING
Jeff Youngquist, VP, Production and Special Projects
Sarah Singer, Editor, Special Projects
Jeremy West, Manager, Licensed Publishing
Sven Larsen, VP, Licensed Publishing
David Gabriel, SVP Print, Sales & Marketing
C.B. Cebulski, Editor in Chief

The publisher is not responsible for websites (or their content) that are not owned by the publisher.

Additional photography credit information is on page 167.

Print book cover and interior design by Justine Kelly

Library of Congress Cataloging-in-Publication Data has been applied for.

ISBNs: 978-0-7624-8580-2 (paperback), 978-0-7624-8660-1 (ebook)

RRD-S

10   9   8   7   6   5   4   3   2   1

★ ★ ★

For my dad and mom, who encouraged
me to follow my dreams.

And all the cosplayers who I can
now call my friends.

★ ★ ★

Photographer Jason Laboy captures TrevRayCosplay in the classic Spidey pose.

CONTENTS

FOREWORD
★ ★ ★   ★ ★ ★

WELCOME TO THE EXTRAORDINARY WORLD OF Marvel Cosplay!

I'm so honored to be writing this foreword for my incredible friend, cosplayer Judy Stephens. Working in Hollywood as a costume designer and shepherding its process from script to screen has been a dream come true for me, but nothing could have prepared me for the unforgettable journey of joining Marvel.

The Marvel Cinematic Universe (MCU) has become a cultural phenomenon for millions of fans where they can revel and rejoice as their iconic super heroes and villains are brought to life. As the costume designer for *Marvel's Agents of S.H.I.E.L.D.* and Marvel Studios' *She-Hulk: Attorney at Law*, I've experienced firsthand the magic of transforming actors into these beloved characters.

But it's not just on screen that the Marvel Universe comes alive; it's in the hearts and minds of fans, like you, who are drawn to the rich storytelling, complex characters, and immersive worlds that Marvel has created. For many, this experience has opened a door to a new way of expressing your love for these characters, through the art of cosplay.

Cosplay is a form of self-expression and performance art where fans create their own highly detailed costumes in honor of their favorite characters from movies, television, comic books, and pop culture. It's a labor of love that requires fierce creativity, dedication, and craftsmanship. One of the most rewarding aspects of my journey in the cosplay community has been my friendship with Judy.

Judy and I met on the set of *Agents of S.H.I.E.L.D.*, where we bonded over our mutual admiration for the intricate details of Marvel costumes. We continued to debate the merits of different materials

and techniques, while cheering each other on as we brought our own costumes to life. My official initiation into the world of cosplay was at the 2014 San Diego Comic-Con (SDCC) when Judy invited me to join the "Women of Marvel" panel. That experience was a life-changing moment for me, because it was the first time that I was able to meet cosplayers of *Agents of S.H.I.E.L.D.* I was not only humbled by their unfettered love for the show and its characters, but also by the authentic dedication they had applied to their costumes. I realized then that cosplay has the power to transform not only the creator-wearer but also those who witness it.

After that, I jumped at the chance to judge the Crown Championships of Cosplay at the Chicago Comic & Entertainment Expo (C2E2) in 2015. It was there that I learned how intensely beautiful and imaginative the world of cosplay can be: from the

Ann with fellow Woman of Marvel Margaret Stohl after judging the costume contest at New York Comic Con (NYCC) in 2015.

unique take on a favorite character, to the varied use of materials, to the love and commitment to build. I remember seeing a costume at C2E2 that took years to build, the gorgeous handwork, connecting thousands of tiny brass hoops by hand to create an elaborate gored chainmail full skirt. Throughout the years, cosplayers have continually left me in a state of awe and admiration.

In this book, you'll find a wealth of information and inspiration to help you create your own Marvel-inspired cosplay. Judy will take you behind the scenes of the creative process, from choosing the right character and planning your costume to mastering the techniques of sewing, prop-making, makeup, and posing. Most notably, this book goes beyond just the technical aspects of cosplay. It also highlights the joy of self-expression, the empowerment of embodying a beloved character, and the sense of community that comes with being part of the Marvel cosplay fandom. Cosplay has the power to boost self-confidence, unleash creativity, and help you form lasting connections with like-minded fans who share our love for Marvel.

Marvel cosplay is a celebration of diversity, inclusion, and acceptance. It's a world where anyone, regardless of their age, gender, body type, or background, can become a hero—or a villain—and be celebrated for their unique interpretation of these iconic characters.

Happy cosplaying!

ANN FOLEY
COSTUME DESIGNER

LEFT: Ann with cosplayers after judging the costume contest at NYCC in 2015.
RIGHT: Ann Foley sitting on the "Women of Marvel" panel at SDCC 2015.

AS I SIT HERE, HOME FROM MY 110TH CONVENTION, cosplay props hanging on the bookcase, and my cats curled up in the leftover fabric piled on my ironing board, I am excited to share with you this *hobby* that has fueled my creativity, relationships, and career for most of my adult life.

My name is Judy Stephens, and I humbly call myself a *cosplay wrangler*. For more than fifteen years, I have been the go-to person for cosplay at Marvel. But, even before my first day working at Marvel in 2006, cosplay was already a part of my life. Thanks to high school friends, I was introduced to anime and manga, which then led me to American comics. And it was after my freshman year of college, in 2004, that I attended my first convention in Toronto, Canada. Anime North was small then, only about 8,500 attendees, but still loud, colorful, and just . . . *incredible*. With my film camera in hand (a Nikon N80 my dad purchased for my six-teenth birthday), I clicked away, capturing moments from the convention floor and cosplay gatherings. I may not have known it then, but I was *hooked*.

Born and raised in metro Detroit, I was lucky to have a mother who not only knew how to sew, but had made countless outfits for herself and others, even sewing her sister's wedding dress—1980s puffed sleeves and all. This would guarantee me a childhood filled with homemade Halloween costumes, and then when I showed interest, an introduction to the craft. The first thing I learned was how to darn my socks. And then from there, with ironing assistance, napkins. There were multiple Christmases where every family member was gifted with slightly crooked napkins.

As a teenager, with my first foray into fandom, I would ask my mother to sew my first cosplay—though it was years before I knew that word. After seeing

Kris Anka's updated Captain Marvel uniform from 2016.

Costume Contest judges Susie Creates (as Captain Marvel) and Michael Burson (as Doctor Strange) pose at the Marvel booth.

Cosplay is a form of self-expression and performance art where fans create their own highly detailed costumes in honor of their favorite characters from movies, television, comic books, and pop culture.

Judy and Sana Amanat hosting a "Women of Marvel" panel at San Diego Comic-Con.

Titanic in theaters thirteen times (yes, you read that right), my mom made me one of Rose's dresses. I still have it today, packed away in the closet, even though I'll never be able to fit into it again. But it wouldn't be until college that I began to make my own.

After that first convention in 2004, I knew we had to go back the next year, and I had to bring a costume. Those early ones were . . . rough, to say the least, but we all have to start somewhere. Over the years I would continue to build on each skill I learned, from new stitches and sewing different materials, to working with wigs and the early foam options. A certificate in millinery (hat making) from the Fashion Institute of Technology helped me develop my patterning and building techniques. Plus, the countless forum tips, how-to guides, and now video walk-throughs: each piece helped me become the cosplayer I am today.

And I did return to Anime North in 2005. From there I began discovering new conventions each year from Otakon to Katsucon to New York Anime Fest (now a part of New York Comic Con). Eventually I built

up my confidence to ask cosplayers if I could take their photos. After joining LiveJournal, managing a cosplay photo booth, and building a community of cosplayers, I became one of the few female (and on demand) cosplay photographers in the scene.

By this time, I had been hired by Marvel as an intern (February 2006), next as a temp, and finally full-time as a graphic designer (January 2008). Over the following years, I was promoted from designer to project manager to finally producer. And like many others at Marvel, with our multiple hats, I would become the official photographer for conventions and events, and the unofficial cosplay wrangler. If you've been to the Marvel booth at San Diego Comic-Con or New York Comic Con, you've likely seen me running around onstage, photographing. (And when I wasn't doing all my actual jobs, I also co-created and produced the *Women of Marvel* podcast.)

Since then, I have likely taken more than a half-million photos at conventions, and of that 100,000 of just cosplay. And in my time at Marvel, I produced *Marvel*

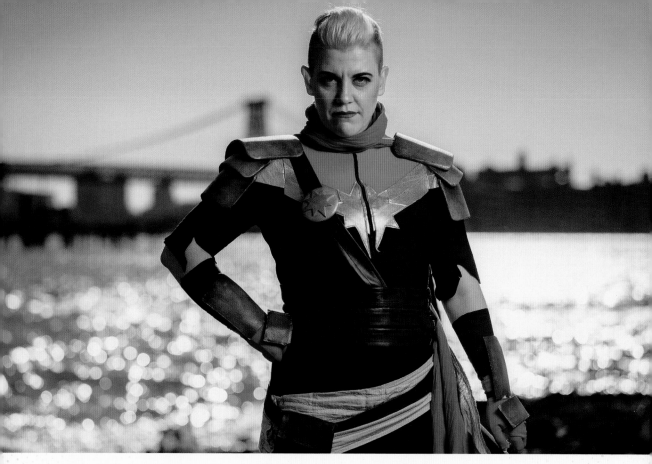

Judy poses for photographer Carlos Adama in her apocalyptic Captain Marvel with the NYC skyline in the background.

Becoming, Marvel Cosplay Covers, and Costoberfest, while each year organizing the Marvel costume contests at conventions. And most recently I assisted in casting for Marvel's 616-episode *Suit Up* on Disney+. All these years of cosplay, creating, working, and celebrating in this space have led up to this book.

Now twenty years later, I've made more than thirty costumes, many of them of Marvel characters, including Captain Marvel and Mystique. Just a month after the release of the first issue of *Captain Marvel* with Carol Danvers in 2012, I debuted my first version of her at Dragon Con.

Now, as cosplay has become a popular element of fandom, I have the honor to write Marvel's first book celebrating cosplay. Featuring just a few representatives of the incredibly diverse cosplay community, we'll introduce you to the skills you can use to build your own Marvel costumes. And then with your new costume, wig styled, and shield in hand, you'll be ready to join us at a convention to pose for your first photo on the Marvel stage!

For the last two decades, I've been lucky to be a part of this welcoming community, doing my small part advocating for its celebration by the brands we love. Just like I was all those years ago, you'll find yourselves hooked by cosplay. I am so happy you are all here to join me on this adventure. Buckle up as we get ready to go higher, further, and faster!

PART I

WELCOME TO COSPLAY!

★ ★ ★

CHAPTER 1

The Story of Marvel and Cosplay

★ ★ THE ORIGINS OF COSPLAY ★ ★

FIRST OF ALL, I'D LIKE TO WELCOME YOU TO COSPLAY! This magical world is built from a community supporting and celebrating a passion for dressing up as your favorite character. It began as a niche, tiny world, and over the years has grown into a phenomenon and staple of convention culture, from comic to science fiction and fantasy. Before we dive into the many ways to explore and interact with cosplay and the community, let's first go back to its origins.

Although the idea of costuming, or dressing up as a fictional character, has long been written into our history as humans, cosplay is much younger. Even the word "cosplay" itself is technically only a millennial—the word just turned a youthful forty. For context, this book's author is about the same age. And I am *still* cosplaying!

A Japanese play on words, *cosplay* was first printed in June 1983 by the Japanese writer Nobuyuki Takahashi to describe his experience seeing fans in costume at a Tokyo convention. He referred to what they were doing as "cosplay," blending the words *costume* and *play* together. The article in *My Anime* refers to both costume play (コスチュームプレー, kosuchuumu puree) and cosplay (コスプレ, kosupure). In the 1990s the word became common within the Japanese community, and then it crossed the ocean.

By the time the term landed in the United States, fans had been wearing costumes to science fiction conventions since their early days in the 1930s. You can trace this through the decades as science fiction TV shows, like *Star Trek*, became popular. From these early sci-fi conventions, comic fans ran with the idea of this kind of event and branched off to create their own comic-focused shows.

One of those fans was Phil Seuling, who held the first New York Comic Art Convention in 1968. Putting on a convention then (and even now) was a family affair, as his then-wife, Carole Seuling, helped organize most of the show, including the costume events. Carole, who wrote the first incarnation of *Shanna the She-Devil* (and whom I had the honor to speak to for the *Women of Marvel* podcast) regaled me with stories of attending cons in the 1960s and 1970s. When I asked her if fans dressed up, the quick answer was "Of course," as she even made costumes for herself, family, and friends.

Conventions continued to expand in the United States, alongside the beginning of the "modern age" of comic books, with expansion of the X-Men line and rise of the anti-hero. A new generation of comic fans came of age in a timeline of contemporary characters, storylines, and art styles. By the early 1990s, show attendees started totaling over 10,000, with San Diego Comic-Con moving into the now-iconic convention center in 1995, with more than 34,000 attendees. As conventions grew, so did the number of fans attending, wearing their handmade super hero costumes. But for Americans, there was no colloquial word to describe what they were doing.

Back in Japan, fans had embraced the idea, and by the 1990s cosplay had developed into a popular

THE 1969 COMIC·ART CONVENTION LUNCHEON
STATLER·HILTON HOTEL   JULY 5, 1969

Attendees of New York Comic Fest in 1969.

activity. Fans would dress up as their favorite characters from anime, manga, and early video games. By the 1980s, anime had gained traction with the release of *Gundam, Dragon Ball,* and films by Studio Ghibli.

Just as the West had adopted the idea of costuming, the East exported their animation right to the front of the minds of young soon-to-be fans across America. Many of those early cosplayers look back to those first dubbed anime series, which were interspersed between American cartoons, as their gateway to cosplay. Along with the Japanese exports of anime and manga, the idea of cosplay was introduced to a new generation of fans, expanding who or what you could dress up as at a convention.

By the time the calendar flipped into the new century, anime conventions were spreading across the United States with young fans stepping onto the floor in their very first cosplays. In her book *Yaya Han's World of Cosplay,* cosplayer Yaya Han talks about her experience first attending a convention in 1999. Seeing real people dressed up as the characters she had grown to love, she realized, "This is what I wanted to do." Just like Yaya, I was one of those fans, and similar to many of my friends, my early costumes were created from a mix of found items from the closet, such as a prom skirt, or a top sewn by my mother.

In those early years, most costumes were made with found items, or if you learned to sew, whatever material you could find at the local fabric store. The characters you chose likely had the same color hair as you, or what you could find on eBay, as wig options were scarce. The more adventurous read a tutorial on cosplay.com about how to dye a wig with a permanent marker bath.

Looking back to the 2000s, there certainly were no EVA foams or thermoplastics (if you don't recognize these words, don't worry; we'll explain in the next chapter!), so armor was either made of cardboard or something ridiculously complicated like vacuum forming plastic. I still remember the first 3D-printed cosplay armor I saw at a convention around 2010. It was incredible! But we were still years away from 3D printing becoming more accessible and a common aspect of cosplay.

That period of time in the early part of this century highlighted the ingenuity of cosplayers, but also showcased how we came together as a community to support others who were learning new skills. By the time I started, in 2004, the foundation of what would become the now-standard video tutorials had begun to form. On sites like cosplay.com, LiveJournal, and DeviantArt, a cosplayer could find threads or image guides walking them through making a costume or prop. These forums easily spread the wealth of information, plus they also allowed cosplayers to meet fellow fans of the newest show or game—which then would progress to meeting in person at a convention, and maybe even cosplaying together.

Those early online connections ignited lifelong friendships, and even relationships, between cosplayers across the world. From one post in 2006 on cosplay.com's forum, I met my best friend; we've been friends for almost twenty years.

Now it's social media, or even convention-specific apps, that allow fans to connect for meetups or to just share their newest cosplay. But it was the birth and spread of Facebook and then Instagram that tracked the growth of cosplay from niche fandom to today's worldwide community.

World-renowned cosplayer Yaya Han has made over 400 costumes, including many Marvel characters.

★ ★ COSPLAY AND ITS SUBCULTURE ★ ★

Now, we all know cosplay has become an established element of fandom. But it really required the right things coming together. For comics, the 1980s and early 1990s were a booming time, with *X-Men #1*, published in 1991, selling more than 8 million copies. But what goes up must come down, and by the end of the decade, the comic bubble had burst.

So, by the 2000s, comics were finally finding their feet again, especially at Marvel, with stories, like *Civil War*, that hit the social temperature, and new and distinctly different-looking characters, like in *The Runaways*. For the first time in over a decade, comics were becoming *cool* again, and this time with new readers. At the same time was the emergence of what we now know as social media. Marvel was an

The Marvel photo shoot at Dragon Con would break out from one set of stairs to many, highlighting the expanding universes and characters.

early adopter—then Marvel.com editor Ryan Penagos joined Twitter in 2007 with the now well-known @AgentM handle. It was Ryan, and the following social media managers, who expanded Marvel's presence online from forums to Tumblr, Instagram, TikTok, and the ever-evolving new social platforms.

Before this, the cosplay community had grown during the age of message boards: LiveJournal and DeviantArt. Now with the rise of social platforms it became easier to connect and grow an audience to share your cosplay with.

Then in 2008, Marvel Studios' *Iron Man* was released. Almost immediately a new door was opened for cosplayers. I don't want to give all the credit to Marvel Studios for how cosplay exploded, but the Marvel films certainly helped spread the fandom of super heroes to the cosplay community and beyond. Truly, it became a worldwide phenomenon.

With the explosion of popularity for cosplay, the final piece of the puzzle fell into place: *accessibility*. In the beginning, cosplay required learning new skills, from sewing to crafting, but now it's no longer

a requirement; cosplay is easier than ever. If you're not ready to build a full super hero suit, you can get started with an entry-level form of cosplay, such as closet cosplay (adapting clothes and props found in your closet) to bounding (mixing owned and purchased items to assemble an outfit inspired by your favorite character) or even purchasing a fully ready-to-go costume online. Closet cosplay has been around for a bit, owing to cosplayers looking for a casual and cost-effective way of adding to their costume repertoire. *Bounding* was coined by a group of Disney fans about a decade ago and has now spread throughout many other fandoms.

From there, if you want to try your hand at sewing, the tools are right at your fingertips: from Yaya Han's cosplay-specific fabrics and patterns at Joann Fabrics to foam and thermoplastics available at Blick Art Materials and high-quality costumes available for purchase online. No more hand-coloring a wig with a Sharpie, as now a quick search on Amazon will find one. And you don't need to save your cardboard, as 3D printing has changed the armor game. Plus, forum

4

tutorials have evolved into full video walk-throughs on YouTube or Twitch.

Born from those early niche sci-fi and anime conventions, cosplay now has become a culture on its own. Conventions are the perfect place where these new fans can go to share in this burgeoning passion. By the 2010s, there was likely a convention every weekend, even multiple across the country. Just like back in 1984 at Worldcon, cosplayers needed a place to share their new costumes. These shows grew from a few thousand attendees to more than 150,000, at San Diego Comic-Con, and in 2019, New York Comic Con had more than 260,000 attendees across the four-day convention.

Another prominent show for cosplay is Dragon Con, which was launched in 1987 in Atlanta, Georgia. That first year they had 1,400 attendees, but by the late 2010s they were quickly approaching 100,000. The reason I bring up Dragon Con is that it's a show where I've clearly seen how cosplay has expanded, especially for Marvel.

Held over Labor Day weekend, for four days at Dragon Con fans bring the best, biggest, and newest cosplays. It's normal to be walking down the hallway and see a large Avengers group, an incredible Iron Man armor with LEDs, and then an immaculately dressed Drag Queen Storm.

In 2009, the Superhero Costuming Forum hosted their first Marvel Universe gathering with about eighty cosplayers attending. Over the years it grew to the point where, in 2019, we had more than 800 people in costume across two large stairs, and another 500 onlookers. And that was just the one meetup, with options for an X-Men meetup the day before, or a World of Wakanda photo shoot the following day.

Dragon Con is a great example of how, over time, conventions and cosplay have become intricately intertwined; it is now hard to imagine one existing

In addition to the giant photo shoot, there are multiple organized gatherings at Dragon Con, including one for the World of Wakanda.

without the other. Tomorrow if you were to attend a fandom convention, anywhere in the world, from comic to anime to sci-fi, there would be cosplayers there—some would be wearing their hundredth costume and others debuting their first.

Conventions also offer more than just a place to wear your costume. Starting back in the early days of shows, there were costume parade events that evolved into cosplay contests and masquerades, competitions where a skit is judged alongside your cosplay. Beside these events, conventions serve as a way for cosplayers to meet the actors playing their favorite character or the creator who drew the version of the costume they're wearing. Before being online, outside of the comic letter columns and the US post, the only place you could interact with fellow fans, or even wear a costume, was at conventions. With the explosion of the internet, so came an expansion of conventions, the attendees, and those looking to capture it all—the photographers.

In the early days, cosplayers were lucky if there was a photographer at all attending, with many photos captured with a film one-time-use camera. By the mid-2000s, drawn by the buzz of online forums, it became commonplace to be asked by a photographer if they might take your photo. But with the evolution of digital photography, cosplay photography is now synonymous with conventions. As you walk the con floor, it's easy to

Avengers Assemble! A group of Captain America cosplayers strike a pose on the Marvel stage.

spot another attendee capturing a photo of a cosplayer on their phone, or even photographers organizing an elaborate photo shoot. And after you've poured all the blood, sweat, and tears into your newest cosplay, you want to make sure you get a good photo to share online, or even with a fellow fan.

There is also something magical about those interactions in a costume from the same film or comic. At my most recent trip to Dragon Con, I took a moment to step back and just watch as the community came together again. And as cosplay has spread around the world, the everlasting theme is that everyone is welcome, no matter your color, size, age, identity, or skill. It is the passion for cosplay that connects us all.

★ ★ MARVEL CELEBRATES COSPLAY ★ ★

Cosplay has been a part of Marvel's history longer than most people think. There is a famous photo from 1969 of soon-to-be Marvel editor in chief Roy Thomas in a Spider-Man costume posing alongside Stan Lee, classic Marvel comic artist John Romita Sr., and the first female staff artist, Marie Severin—all four of them laughing. And from the late 1960s to the 1970s, Marvel editors and creators would travel up to Rutland, Vermont, for their super hero–themed Halloween parade. Plus, there was the Mighty Marvel Comic Convention in 1975 and 1976. From then on, I'm sure there were fans dressing up at conventions, but it would be more than thirty years, and require the internet, for cosplay to break into the forefront of Marvel fandom.

One of the first photos of a cosplayer on Marvel.com was from New York Comic Con in 2007, likely taken by Marvel's Ryan Penagos. This was an early Marvel forum post, years before there were galleries on the site. Those early photos were just the beginning, with me and other Marvel photographers capturing thousands of photos of cosplayers since.

By the time I attended my first San Diego Comic-Con in 2009, I had become known as "the cosplayer" in the office. So, when a group of Marvel cosplayers approached the booth and asked if they could pose on the stage in front of the *Iron Man* armor, the booth staff sent them to me to manage. It was an early moment, but I knew something was brewing, and that we should be sharing this on Marvel.com.

That was the beginning of Marvel embracing cosplay. With the support of my boss and the Marvel.com editorial team, I set out to showcase cosplayers around the world. The early days were filled with monthly forum posts about a cosplayer or photographer, or even photos from a Marvel meetup at a convention. One profile prompted a photographer, Jay Tablante, to travel from the Philippines to New York City to meet us in person. Jay's day job was in commercial photography, but for fun he worked with a team to capture incredible super hero photos of cosplayers. I was even treated to a *super* photo in my Captain Marvel costume. Eventually, by 2011, the forums evolved into actual articles and galleries on a newly launched Marvel.com.

And with the success of the first Marvel Costume Contest in 2009 at New York Comic Con, the event would return to each convention, growing bigger and better. From SDCC to NYCC to C2E2, the costume contest became one of the must-sees at the Marvel booth (well, besides the surprise celebrity appearances). It was held as the last event during Saturday's programming; fans arrived early to get a good spot to see cosplayers walk and pose on the stage.

7

Blending her Captain Marvel suit and bomber jacket, cosplayer Morgan Duhon poses for the camera.

Tomorrow if you were to attend a fandom convention, anywhere in the world, from comic to anime to sci-fi, there would be cosplayers there—some would be wearing their hundredth costume and others debuting their first.

For many entering, there was a hope to win the grand prize, but for others, it was an opportunity to show off their Marvel costumes and meet fellow Marvel fans.

If you couldn't make the costume contest, there were other events to don cosplays for. There were the Marvel Cosplay Photo Ops, the Kids' Costume Event, and the many opportunities to get a photo with your favorite comic creator or actor. Plus, even stopping by the booth you were likely to have a Marvel staff member stop you to grab your photo, or even get invited onstage by the official photographer. And from there, you had something to show off to all your friends: your cosplay marked with the iconic Marvel.com watermark.

In these early days, very few brands, let alone one of the big two in comics, were highlighting cosplay like Marvel was. And in between conventions, we'd ask fans to submit photos of themselves in cosplay for events like Captain America's seventy-fifth

anniversary, Avengers vs. X-Men, or Costoberfest. (Blending cosplay and Oktoberfest, Costoberfest was a month of cosplay celebration across Marvel.com and our social channels.)

And then in 2015, Marvel released the first of two comic variant programs: Marvel Cosplay Covers. These twenty-one variants, essentially comic books printed with different, unique covers, featured cosplayers from across the United States, including Iron Man, Ms. Marvel, Groot, and more. It was such a success that an additional fourteen covers were released in 2016. For many of the cosplayers, who had grown up reading and collecting comics, it was a dream come true to now be on an actual cover.

By 2016, what is now called the Marvel Digital Media Team was tasked to launch a collection of new video series for Marvel.com and YouTube. And thus, *Marvel Becoming* was born. With the help of

TOP: Jay Tablante's cosplay photography featuring Riki "Riddle" LeCotey.

BOTTOM: An Iron Man cosplayer poses onstage at New York Comic Con.

Merly the cosplay dog poses with her owner, Amanda, at San Diego Comic-Con.

cosplayers from New York to Atlanta, including some allowing me to sleep on a few couches, the first season simply showcased cosplayers in Marvel costumes. From there, each season we stepped up our game—including making-of moments, interviews, and beautiful cosplay poses. *Marvel Becoming* highlighted the diversity of cosplay in color, age, size, skill level, and cosplay origin story. It also encompassed every type of Marvel content, from comics to video games to films and TV. The video series became just one more way to welcome new fans into the cosplay community.

From those early days, cosplay and fandom have been a part of Marvel's story. It has become common, though still thrilling, to see cosplayers everywhere from conventions to social media to posing on the red carpet at a film's premiere. And now it's your turn to join in. You've learned about the history of cosplay; now it's time to learn how to cosplay!

Strut Your Stuff at the Marvel Cosplay Contests

★ ★ ★

Since the early days of conventions there have always been some type of costume contests or events, with Marvel jumping in headfirst with their first officially documented one at New York Comic Con in 2008. Before there was the epic stage and LED screen, fans huddled around twenty-five or so cosplayers posed before a table of judges, who were all Marvel employees. From that moment on, the contest became an honored tradition at every show, spreading to San Diego Comic-Con and then C2E2 and WonderCon.

On Saturday evening, after the insanity of various Marvel Studios signings was over, fans crowded into the booth for the best spot to see which marvelous cosplay would win. The judges evolved from any employee who was hanging out to costume designers, like Ann Foley, and famous cosplayers, such as Yaya Han and CutiePieSensei. And from those first twenty-five costumes, it expanded to a stage full of cosplayers, with one year at NYCC having more than a hundred entrants.

Throughout the double-digit events, from first-time cosplayers and adorable children to epic costumes, the experience of the crowd cheering each cosplayer on as they strut across the stage never gets old.

ABOVE: Friends in both comics and real life, a Captain Marvel and Ms. Marvel cosplay duo poses at the end of the New York Comic Con Costume Contest in 2015.

TOP RIGHT: The Nova Corp, from the past to current and even alternate worlds, pose on the Marvel stage at New York Comic Con in 2017.

BOTTOM RIGHT: Straight from the silver screen, the Avengers assemble on the Marvel stage for the New York Comic Con Costume Contest in 2012.

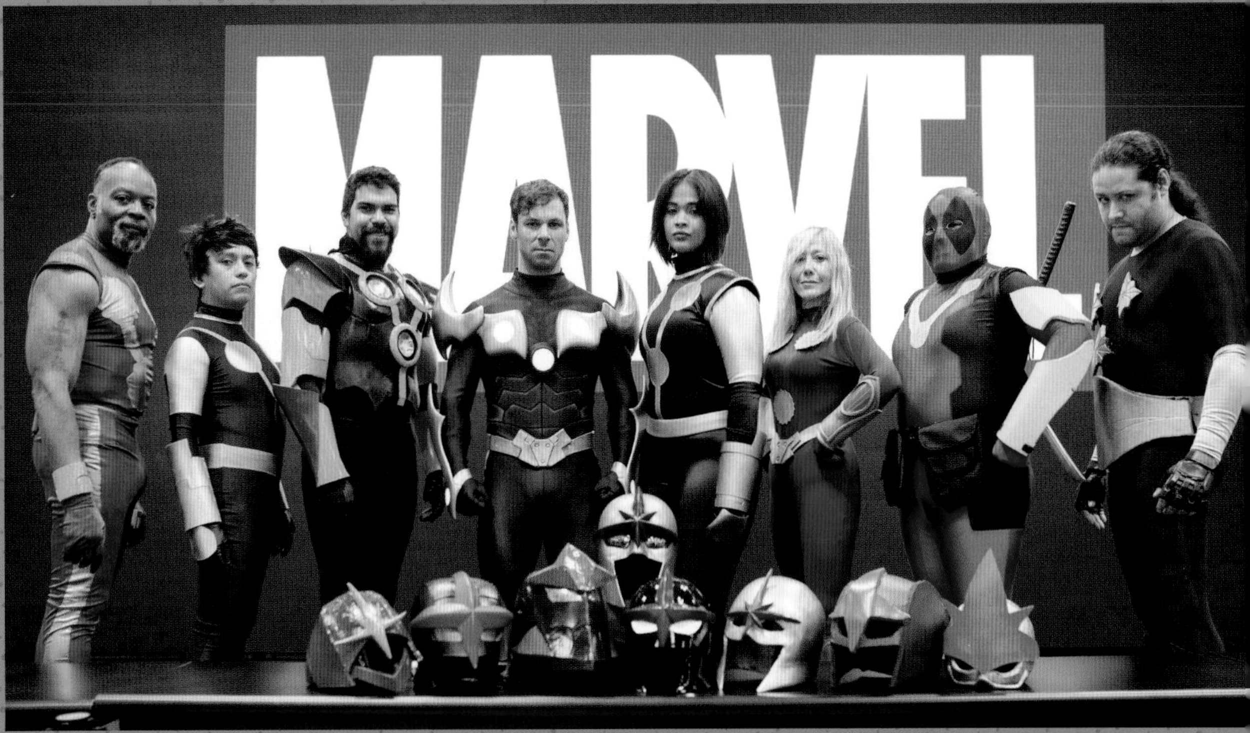
MARVEL

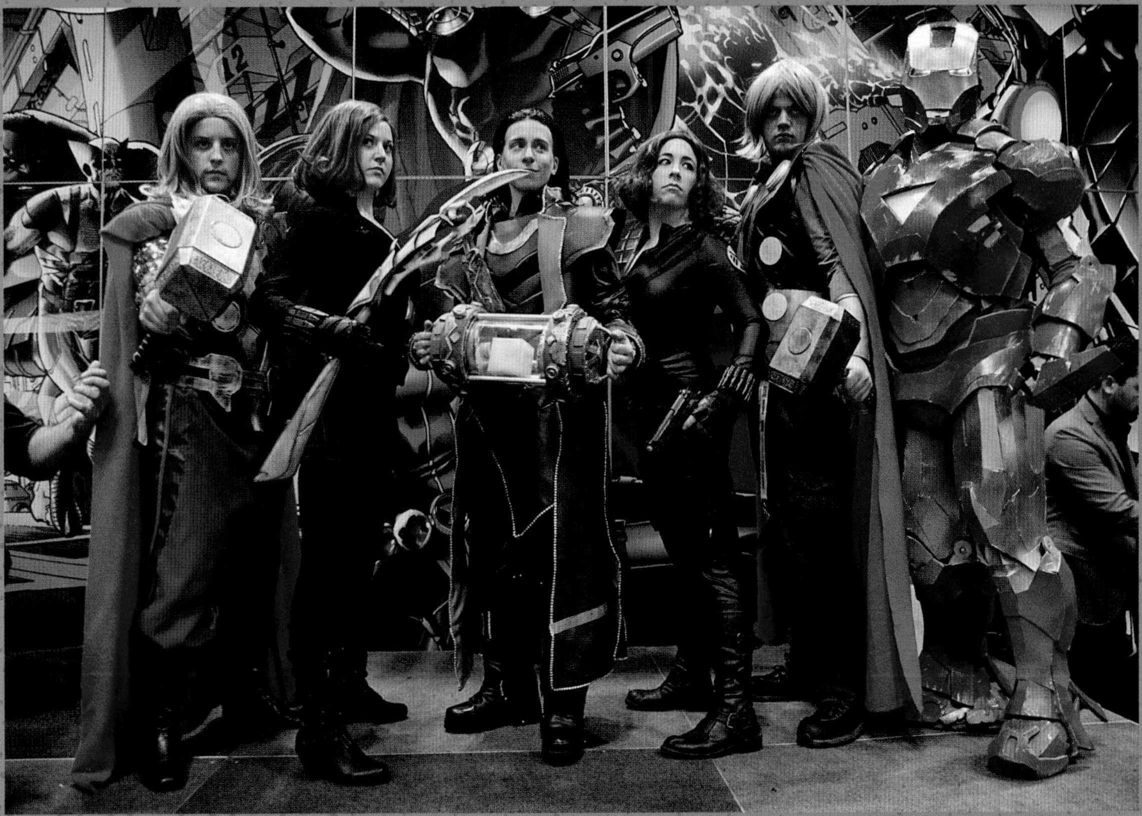

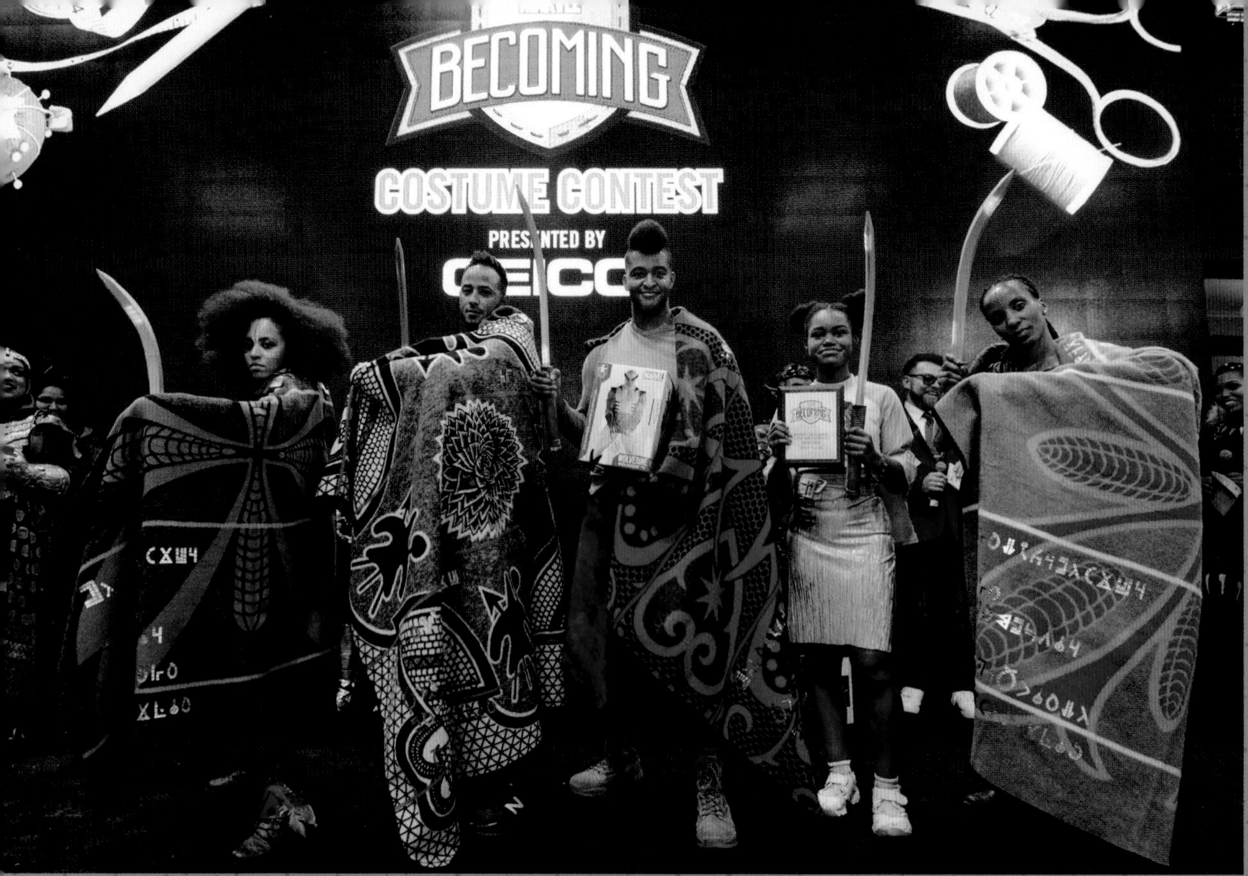
BECOMING
COSTUME CONTEST
PRESENTED BY

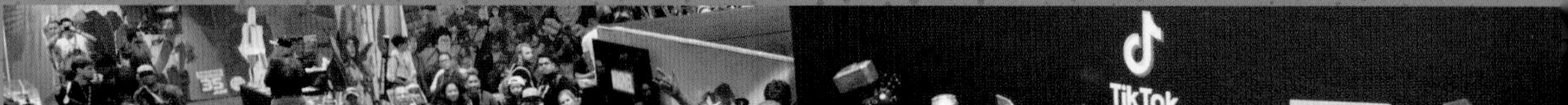
TikTok
THANOS IS A JERK

TOP: Wakanda Forever! The 2019 New York Comic Con Costume Contest winners pose on the stage with their prizes.

BOTTOM: Flashing back to 2019 San Diego Comic-Con cosplayers from across the Marvel Universes.

CHAPTER 2

How to Cosplay

Now that you've learned about the history of cosplay, you may be wondering, "Where do I even begin?" No need to stress, because this book will walk you through each step. We'll first start with your options on how to cosplay, before diving into the tricky decision of what character to cosplay, including research, planning, and finally choosing a design. The adventure awaits you, so let's dive right in!

★ ★ OPTIONS FOR COSPLAY ★ ★

COSPLAY MIGHT HAVE STARTED OUT WITH HANDMADE costumes and accessories, but now cosplayers have a whole host of options and paths to create their looks. Starting off, you can adapt clothes and props found in your closet to create your very first *closet cosplay*, or use a mix of owned and purchased items to assemble an outfit inspired by your favorite character (this is known as bounding). From there, with your toes dipped in, you can begin the process of building a full costume, either crafting by hand or acquiring from another source.

If you want, it is possible to purchase pieces or your whole cosplay online, either from a reputable online costume retailer or by commissioning someone to make it. Just like many previous generations of seamsters, there are now cosplayers who will make costumes for others as their day job. They'll take your measurements, possibly schedule fittings, and craft specific pieces or a fully finished costume for you.

For many cosplayers, it's an easy decision to purchase props or elements of a costume, either 3D printed or custom crafted, to ease the list of to-do's while making a costume. I actually did this for a recent non-Marvel cosplay prop, purchasing a 3D file from

the cosplayer team Dangerous Ladies, and then having Marc Schwerin (Marc and his Loki costume are profiled in chapter 8) print it on his 3D printer, before priming and painting it myself. In the early days, there weren't a lot of options other than to make every element of your cosplay, which was special in its own way; but times have changed, and now, I believe, the best cosplayer uses all the tools and resources at their disposal.

For finding other elements, the internet is your friend, from wigs to shoes to gloves and so much more. If you can find an option on eBay or Amazon, that will likely be your best bet instead of having to create it from scratch or source it locally. I and a few of our cosplayers are lucky to be based in New York, so we do have great options for fabric and accessories, but even then, buying online may be the best option. This is true for props, too. For example, Hasbro has released a series of premium prop replicas under their Marvel Legends line, which could be a great choice for Captain America's shield or Black Panther's helmet.

And then there is what we lovingly call closet cosplay, which is when you use clothing pieces or props that you already own to put together as a costume.

15

This could be a casual look for a comic character, such as a leather jacket and jeans, or adapting a pair of pants or shoes to match the costume. At some point or another, all cosplayers have done this, and many are still doing this. For example, my casual look Carol Danvers is a Her Universe jacket, jeans, and an official Marvel hat. Not one stitch was added. This may be the best approach when you've been invited to a last-minute costuming group, and you now need to assemble a costume a few days before the convention, which mostly ends with you pulling items from your closet and same-day shipping a wig and shoes.

In the same vein, there is also the option of bounding, where you use a mix of owned and purchased items to assemble a fashion outfit inspired by your favorite character. It's basically a cosplay without the costume. Pulling together everyday pieces, such as jean shorts, a pink top, and some eighties sunglasses—*bam*, now you're bounding as Jubilee.

No matter what you decide, cosplay is all about having fun, so test the waters to see what works best for you, from your skill level to budget. But I do hope you give it a try to learn how to sew and craft your own cosplay! There is such a joy in debuting a costume you've worked so hard to make—including the first time you get to say, "Yes, I made this!"

Marjoanofarc wearing a casual Mary Jane cosplay with a red wig, Spider-Man top, and accessories.

★ ★ IT'S RESEARCH TIME! ★ ★

MAYBE IT'S YOUR FAVORITE CHARACTER. OR YOU HAVE the same haircut. Or you've been invited to join an X-Men group at New York Comic Con. Or maybe it's just a good entry point for you to learn the skills. If you have a hero or theme in mind, the first thing to do is research! As many Marvel characters have been around for almost eighty years, there are many, many versions to choose from. Maybe you'll look to start at

the beginning and do the classic Captain America, just like our cosplayer Mark (see page 52). Or maybe you've been inspired by the Hellfire Gala designs by Russell Dauterman and are thinking of creating Rogue's new look.

There are also some incredible fan art cosplay versions out there, from historical takes to unique and playful mashups. A few years ago at San Diego

Comic-Con, there was a comedic group of Avengers whose iconic looks were combined with famous fast-food brands. Remember, there is really no limit to where you take cosplay. No matter who you are, you can cosplay and certainly do it however you can and want to. At its core, cosplay is a way to share your passion for a fandom, and throughout the decades, fans have used the costumes they've worn to connect with this incredible community, along the way learning a few things about themselves.

Now that you have a character chosen, it's time to let your fingers do the work and find reference images in the comics or online. It's always helpful to have as many images from as many different sources as you can find, and you'll want to make sure there are good high-res images of the front but also of the back. What are the details on the belt or the prop? Can you tell what shoes the character is wearing? You'll want to save each image and any other resources for when you need to break down the cosplay into colors and patterns, and start thinking about how to assemble each element. Also, it's helpful to have these on hand when you're shopping for fabric and other important pieces for your look.

Another option is to see if other cosplayers have also created a cosplay of your chosen character. This can be incredibly valuable, because their cosplay can give you ideas about the materials, modifications, and process behind how they put it all together or perhaps inspire you to do things differently. The trickiest thing about 2D characters when you are trying to make something 3D is that the character is not always realistically drawn in both form and function.

Cosplayers come in all shapes, sizes, and abilities, so while doing your research you may even luck out and discover a cosplayer has posted a tutorial or even a pattern that you can use to save some time. I was spoiled with the last few cosplays I've made, because

Costuming can run the gamut, from historical fashion to bunny suits, and there are many routes you can take with your cosplay, like binkxy in her Loki variant.

I was able to purchase instructional elements to help guide me as I crafted, including the specific materials the cosplay used and the process they used to add details. For me, these tutorials have saved me a ton of time and stress, as I've been able to follow a set of directions instead of figuring everything out on my own, which means I could spend more time working on personalizing different elements of my cosplay.

CodenameCitadel demostrates how you can pair a custom-printed spandex suit with a helmet and pair of wings.

★ ★ PLANNING A COSPLAY BUILD ★ ★

THE OPTIONS FOR WHICH COSPLAY YOU'D LIKE TO make are truly limitless, especially with the right skills, tools, schedule, and budget. Depending on where and when you'd like to wear your cosplay, you may need to get creative with how you plan to build out the costume. As you begin to plan it out, there are a few things to keep in mind to help you on the path of success.

FIRST QUESTION IS LOCATION.

Where are you going to wear your cosplay? Is this for next year's Halloween to wow all your coworkers with your new crafting expertise, or is it for an upcoming convention? Depending on the time of the year and the location, certain outfits or types of fabrics might not be the most comfortable. For example, you may not want to make a costume with heavy fabric for a convention in August in Atlanta. Another thing to think about is function and movement. If you're going to finally finish that full Iron Man suit, stairs or even just sitting might be your greatest foes. Also, please keep in mind that you'll need to eat, drink, and use the bathroom in your cosplay.

WHAT IS YOUR TIMELINE?

Once you've started thinking about your character and narrowing down the type of cosplay you might be doing, you'll want to consider how much time you have to complete your creation before your event. Are you a great planner and thinking about your cosplay six months before the convention, or are you—like me—working with more of a one- to two-month window? Are there new skills you need to learn, and thus need extra time, or have you made something similar before and have the pattern ready to go?

Thinking about the location, function, and timing should always be a positive aspect of your planning process and shouldn't prevent you from creating the cosplay of your dreams. The best way to make sure you're not stressed out and crafting the night before you leave, or even on the floor of the hotel at the convention, is to answer these questions and then create a build schedule and materials list. I like to work with some padding, to see if my idea is doable, or if I will need to leave some stuff for next time. And as you work through the building process, it's always a good idea to take stock of what you have left and reevaluate your schedule.

KEEP YOUR BUDGET IN MIND.

Cosplay can certainly be pricey, especially when you are hoping to add a new tool to your arsenal or when that perfect fabric you can't stop thinking about is fifteen dollars a yard. So, it's a good idea to make a budget and try to stick to it, as costs add up quickly if you aren't paying attention.

Budgets vary from one cosplayer to another and even from one costume to another, but you'll want to plan on purchasing fabrics, notions, props, wigs, and shoes as well as the finishing touches (makeup, shapewear, jewelry). For example, with a standard super hero suit at 2024 prices, a yard of spandex will run you about $12, and you'll likely need two to three yards for the build. Add on $10 for notions, including a zipper and thread. Then $40 each for a wig and shoes. With just the essential items, the budget is already more than $125.

But don't worry: I have some handy tricks to cut costs! First, try to use scrap fabric for any mockups, lining, or detailing when making your costume or accessories. Second, accessories, like wigs and shoes, and shapewear are easily repurposed from previous costumes. Third, whether you are making or buying your cosplay, always make a list of the exact items you need at the store so you don't get overly excited and buy more thread or a zipper or that extra piece that you don't need. Also keep an eye on your local online cosplay group for any item or fabric swaps, or coupons for your local fabric store. Remember, for most, this is a hobby, so paying the essential bills should come before cosplay.

DO YOU NEED TO LEARN NEW TECHNIQUES?

Think about the techniques involved in your cosplay, including your comfort level with the different skills you might need. You may not know the answer to all these questions just yet, which is totally fine; you'll learn as you build your cosplay library. So now, armed with your chosen cosplay, your build plan, and your budget, it's time to get started gathering the tools and materials you need!

Brett Yee shows off his Sentinel cosplay on the set of Marvel Becoming.

CHAPTER 3

Building Your Cosplay Toolbox!

Since the beginning of human society, we have been passing down the knowledge on how to assemble clothing, from early animal skins to hand weaving. Now we have an abundance of fabrics, from cottons to polyester to leather, and each material has specific qualities that can be used, and different tools needed to finish your project. From fabric and scissors to foam and glue, here is where you'll learn about the basic tools, materials, and terms you'll need to make the costumes in this book and for future cosplays.

★ ★ SEWING TOOLS AND SUPPLIES ★ ★

Every cosplayer's toolbox is a little different, but below is a list of the tools and supplies I keep on hand for my cosplay projects. When you're starting off you may not need every one, but you'll find that along the way as you build your skills, your list of gear will also grow.

SCISSORS

As an essential tool, one of the more important rules with scissors, besides being safe, is to have multiple pairs—one specifically to cut your fabric, only fabric, and then a different pair to cut anything else. That way your fabric scissors are as sharp as possible, and you're not working with dull blades. After that, the scissors you select are a personal choice. I have a pair of dressmaker shears, which can be resharpened, and then an array of other cutting tools, including a rotary cutter and utility knife. And with any sharp implements, keep your cutting surface in mind and protect it with a self-healing mat or foldable superboard.

NEEDLES

You'll need these both for hand-sewing and your sewing machine, and they come in a wide variety of lengths, thicknesses, and sharpness. I like to have a variety pack available for hand-sewing, as I always end up finding a use for the different sizes. And for your machine, you'll want to make sure you match the right type to your fabric, and it always helps to have backups on hand, just in case you break a needle.

THREAD

Just like fabric, thread comes in a wide variety of materials, from polyester to nylon to cotton, and can be found in a truly limitless number of colors. What you're sewing and your budget will help you determine which kind to purchase. And when choosing a color, I always make sure to bring a swatch of my fabric to match, to blend with the costume, or even add detail. Also, it helps to have a few basic colors on hand, including white, black, and the primary colors (red, yellow, and blue).

MEASURING TOOLS

All seamsters have an army of measuring tools in their toolkit, with the tape measure being at the top of the pile. One of my go-to tools is a flexible, clear plastic

A sewing machine, scissors, thread, pins, and a ruler are a few items to add to your sewing toolkit.

ruler, longer than twelve inches, which allows me to mark seam allowances while still being able to see the material underneath. A neat trick is to drill a hole at one end to draw circles and round shapes.

PINS

There is an array of ways to use straight pins, and like all your tools, a range of options to choose from. The primary uses are to attach a pattern to fabric, hold fabric together before stitching, and to help you finish seams. I tend to prefer the slightly longer pin, with a ball head, which I find easier to manage and which I find stays in the fabric even when moving it around. But keep note of the fabric you're using, as not all fabrics are self-healing, like silk or leather, and are easily marked when using pins.

An alternate option to pins is SEWING CLIPS, which are handy when you're working with shifting pieces or delicate fabric.

PINCUSHION

As the first thing I always misplace is my needle, I have several ways to keep track of needles and pins, from a soft pin cushion—think of the customary tomato-shaped ones—to a trusty magnetic wand. Safety note: if you have small creatures in your home, always keep track of your small, sharp implements.

PATTERNS

Learning how to adapt patterns is one of the best skills a cosplayer has in their arsenal, so I always look to have a collection of basic shapes to reference when working on a new costume. A bodysuit pattern is at the top of that list, along with jacket, pants, and glove options. Also it's fun to pick up cosplay-specific and historical costuming patterns.

SEWING MACHINE

This is one of the more important tools in my sewing arsenal. There are many options out there, but they all do the same job, just with more features as you go up in price. Depending on if this is your first purchase or if you're upgrading, there are some great options from an affordable, entry-level machine to more advanced machines with embroidery options. If you can, try visiting a fabric store near you to try out the machines they have on display. You'll get a better idea of the different features, plus even a few tips from the experts. Alternatively, see if you can borrow a family member's or friend's machine, or even purchase a gently used model. Sewing machines can be hardy little things, so one can find itself in many loving homes.

SEWING MACHINE ACCESSORIES

You'll want to make sure to have additional bobbins and a variety of presser feet, like the multi-purpose, zipper, and glide feet.

SERGER

As I work a lot with stretch fabrics, another great tool in my arsenal is a serger. This is an overlocking machine that helps you finish seams, from trimming edges to preventing fraying, and is a great item to have if it's in your budget.

IRON AND IRONING BOARD

One of the tools I put to work through my entire builds is my iron and ironing board. Before even cutting out patterns, I iron the patterns and fabric, and then do so again multiple times throughout sewing, including when finishing seams. The iron also comes in handy if you use fusible interfacing and heat transfer vinyl. Make note of the level of heat you're using on different fabrics and materials, as some may require a pressing cloth to protect from burning or melting.

ADDITIONAL TOOLS

Finally, these are a few additional tools I find helpful to have on hand, including a seam ripper for undoing a sewing mistake, tailor's chalk for marking pattern lines, a thimble for sewing by hand, and finally a box to keep everything organized.

★ ★ THE PATTERN: A SEAMSTER'S BUILDING BLOCKS ★ ★

AS YOUR SEWING TOOL KIT COMES TOGETHER, YOU'LL have to decide which pattern you'll be using for the project. Just like it sounds, a pattern is the blueprint and instructions for you to follow. Patterns can be purchased online or in stores, from large retailers and even from cosplayers themselves. From the early days, cosplayers have always combined a mix of store-bought patterns and at-home drafting. And now brands like McCall's and Simplicity have embraced the hobby and released a wide variety of options to be used by cosplayers, including bodysuits, gloves, boots, and hero-specific looks.

If you are new to cosplay or if this is your first time using a sewing machine, then your best bet is to start working with a store-bought pattern, but as you advance through this book, you can begin to modify and draft your patterns. As with all trades, the more you create, the more you'll start to get a feel of what patterns work for your body, while building a library of ones to use as bases.

If you've purchased a store-bought pattern, in the trusty paper envelope you'll receive the actual printed pattern and instructions. And on the back will be a size chart (make sure you double-check your measurements before purchasing and cutting fabric), a list of suggested fabrics and notions, and the handy table letting you know how much fabric to purchase. Likewise, with each cosplay build in this book, flip to the materials page for a list of what you'll need. With this info in hand, you're ready to tackle fabric shopping.

★ ★ THE MAGIC OF FABRIC SHOPPING ★ ★

IT'S NOW TIME FOR THE FUN PART—FABRIC SHOPPING! Learning about fabric can be a little tricky because there is a vast range of options, and we'll just be touching the surface with this book.

To start with, what are the differences between each type of fabric? At the core is what they are made from, whether it be animal fibers, such as wool from a sheep, or plant fibers, which is how cotton is made. Then there are the synthetic fibers, like polyester. All these fibers can be processed into three different types of fabrics: wovens, knits, and nonwovens. Woven fabrics are the most common and are created on a loom that weaves the fibers together—muslin and denim are included in this group as well—while a knit is constructed by one single yarn interlocked throughout, which helps give the fabric a drape and flow. Finally, faux leather and felt are examples of nonwoven fabrics, which are created by bonding fibers together, giving the fabric a more solid structure. Each has their place and fulfills a specific need, and you'll discover what works best for you and your builds as you create your cosplays.

Still with me? OK, so now you're almost ready to walk into a fabric store and start touching fabrics. The final step is understanding the differences between the many different fabric types. In this book, we're going to focus on those used for our six hero costumes.

SPANDEX

Also commonly called by the brand name Lycra, this is the go-to fabric for super hero costumes because it does what the name suggests: it expands. Spandex is

Views when shopping for fabric in New York City's garment district.

Notions vary from trims to buttons to feathers.

a four-way stretch fabric that is perfect for super suits, leggings, and anything you need to fit tightly. When sewing, you'll want to keep the stretch element in mind, and stitch with a stretch needle and a zigzag stitch.

SATIN

You'll recognize satin for its luxurious shine. It is most commonly used for formal wear and accessories like light, flowing capes and sashes. There are a variety of satins to play with, but some can be a little high maintenance, with a tendency to unravel when sewing and to fray easily.

COTTON

An accessible, easy-to-work-with option, cotton can be used for just about anything. Variants of cotton like muslin and quilting cotton are great options for mockups. But note that, unlike other synthetic materials, cotton offers very little stretch or give in a costume.

LEATHER AND VINYL

Available in animal-based or vegan options, leather and vinyl are the frequent choices for costume accessories, like belts and boots, but can also be used for full costume builds, like a leather jacket. For my Kris Anka Captain Marvel cosplay, I used red leather for all the accessories, including hand-sewn gloves, boot covers, and utility belt and pouches.

I promise, now it's time to head inside the fabric store and start touching fabrics. Really, the best way to choose what will work best—from the feel and structure to the color—is to see it in person. If your only option is ordering online, then take the time to order swatches, which are small squares of the fabric that show off the qualities of the fabric. The more you work with fabric, the more comfortable you'll become in deciding which to pick for different elements as you plan out your future cosplays.

You can't help but be wowed by the details in Beverly Downen's Wasp cosplay suit.

Cosplay can be hard. We all had to begin from somewhere, so don't feel let down if the first attempt isn't perfect or you have a hiccup when you're painting. Sometimes those little mistakes end up teaching you a new technique or even end up creating a better look.

★ ★ THE TOOLS TO FINISH A PROJECT! ★ ★

I DON'T KNOW WHY, BUT I JUST LOVE SHOPPING FOR notions. Granted, I am very spoiled by living in New York City, where we have an abundance of notion stores—and their shop cats. There is something so fun about picking out a colored zipper or choosing the perfect buttons. Although you may be familiar with most of these, as they are likely used on many of the clothes you're wearing, here is a breakdown of the most common elements you'll use:

CLOSURES

These can include buttons, buckles, grommets/eyelets, Velcro, hooks and eyes, magnets, snaps, and zippers. Each of these helps secure the garment or armor to your body. Most sewing machines come with an option to stitch a buttonhole, plus specific feet for sewing in zippers. When shopping for zippers, consider which works best for your build, as there is a considerable variety of styles, lengths, colors, and materials. I typically buy a zipper a little longer than needed as it's easy enough to shorten a zipper using a sewing machine. In addition, many of these types of closures can be used to provide added detail, such as nonfunctioning buckles or intricate buttons.

ELASTIC

It's likely you're currently wearing something with elastic; basically, it allows fabric to stretch and fit a part of your body. As with all notions, the options for elastics are fairly broad, with many widths and colors, and it can be used on the inside of a project for structure or on the outside for design. Also, elastic is your friend when you need a way to attach armor or to wear masks and headpieces.

BIAS TAPE

A great option for finishing edges! Bias tape is a pre-cut and pre-folded strip of fabric that can easily be stitched on to a garment. I'm sure you've seen the packages at your local craft store, including many options for width and colors. If you can't find something that matches, you can make your own bias tape using your costume's fabric or what you have on hand. There are a few tutorials online, but it's easy enough to measure it out, cut, fold, and then iron. If you find yourself making a ton of bias tape, pick up a tape maker to assist.

INTERFACING

Available in either sewable or fusible, interfacing helps strengthen and stabilize fabrics used in a project. You'll see it used mostly in collars, cuffs, and waistbands, but it's also perfect for bodices and capes. I've also used it to help add weight to an appliqué, like Captain Marvel's iconic star, which sits on the front of the costume.

IRON-ON ADHESIVE

One of the newer tools for sewing is HeatnBond, a double-sided iron-on adhesive. This has changed the game for fusing fabrics, foam, and other materials without having to stitch anything. Available in strips or rolls and a variety of weights, HeatnBond is a great tool for appliqué, covering foam with fabric, or even helping sew on a zipper. Also in the same family is vinyl adhesive, an even more modern accessory, which can be cut using a cutting machine or by hand.

LINING

The innermost fabric, a lining helps provide a polished finish and conceals any seams, interfacing, or construction details. It can also serve to add structure to a garment, or for coverage with a thin and transparent fabric. As it's likely the fabric that will touch your skin, you'll want to use a soft, comfortable material, such as cotton, muslin, or even satin. For some super hero costumes, especially ones made with spandex, a lining is usually not required. But if you're looking to enter a cosplay competition or one day sell your costume, a lining is a great way to finish it.

Basically, look to each of these materials to assist in completing your build. Your pattern will suggest the best notions to use, but you can certainly substitute depending on your budget, schedule, or any modifications. Also, as I said above, most of these elements are designed to be hidden, but can be used to add detail to a finished garment.

Speaking of adding detail, as you advance in your skills, you can also consider trim, beading, appliqué, and embroidery (which can be added by hand or machine). Looking forward, you'll see a few of these techniques applied in the upcoming chapters, plus a more thorough breakdown in chapter 9. Now with fabric and notions in hand, it's time to prep your pattern, cut your fabric, and begin sewing.

★ ★ GETTING TO KNOW SEWING TERMS ★ ★

With every profession or hobby, there are terms that are used in tutorials and patterns and in this book. With understanding of these under your belt, you'll be ready to plug in your sewing machine, switch it on, and get ready to press the foot for your first stitch.

FASHION FABRIC
The main fabric for your costume.

RIGHT SIDE/WRONG SIDE
You'll want to pay attention to which side of the fabric you're using as all fabrics have a "right" side and a "wrong" side. The right side is always what is meant to be shown, while the wrong side is what will face the body. When making any marks on fabric, make sure they're on the wrong side so they won't be seen on the final product.

BIAS
For woven fabrics, the bias is the diagonal across the grain, allowing the fabric to stretch. Some pattern pieces are recommended to be cut on the bias, which will help the piece fit to your body.

GRAIN LINE
Essentially, the grain line is the weave of the fabric, showing which direction the threads are running. In each pattern, you'll see an arrow representing the position in which to place each piece on the fabric.

SEAM ALLOWANCE
This is the area of fabric between the seam edge and the stitching line. Standard seam allowance is around ¼ to ½ inch, but you can add or subtract depending on your project. And when drafting or modifying your own patterns, don't forget to add seam allowance; otherwise, it's likely your costume will not fit.

The Hela costume was Beverly's first large build, using a wide variety of tools, including fabric, foam, and silicone.

NOTCHES

Either plain slashes or triangular-shaped wedges added at specified locations along the seam edge. These help keep track of pattern pieces, plus help you match up when pinning and stitching pieces together.

TOPSTITCHING

A visible line of thread sewn on the top of a fabric, most often used for decoration.

THREE GOOD RULES TO FOLLOW FOR ALL COSPLAYERS:

1. Measure twice, cut once.

2. Mockups, mockups, mockups!

3. Try on the pieces as you sew.

LEVELING UP YOUR COSTUME WITH FOAM, 3D PRINTING, AND MORE!

NOW THAT YOU'RE LEVELING UP TO BECOME A SEWING pro, it's time to learn about the crafting element of cosplay—the armor, props, and accessories. Depending on the costume, these aren't always necessary, but as you advance your cosplay game, these skills will be great additions to your repertoire.

THE INFINITE OPTIONS WITH EVA FOAM

First off, just as in the sewing section, this will only be a toe-dip into the immense amount of information for crafting armor and props. For example, *Marvel Becoming* cosplayer Beverly Downen wrote a whole book about how to work with EVA foam—one of the best tools now available in the cosplay crafting community.

Without getting into the scientific side of things, EVA foam is basically a thermoplastic, which is a lightweight and affordable material that is easy to manipulate with heat, and that can be shaped into many, many different forms. I've used it for simple things like providing shape in fabric to the base of arm bracers. But it can also be used for full armor sets, swords, and even space guns.

EVA foam has been around for a while now, but it's only in the last decade that cosplayers realized its possibilities. Early on, it was mostly available from hardware stores for use as floor matting. I'm sure there were plenty of hilarious conversations with cosplayers telling store employees why they were buying so much of the stuff. But it became more commonplace, as cosplayers and then craft stores got into the business. Now you can purchase Yaya Han's foam at Joann or SKS Props' at Blick, including the traditional foam rolls, plus unique shapes, and moldable foam clay. And as you start the planning for your cosplay, you'll have the option of choosing from different thicknesses, colors, levels of density, and more. The options are almost limitless!

Foam, Worbla, paint, and sealant are easily found online or at your local craft stores.

WORKING WITH EVA FOAM

EVA foam is generally considered nontoxic, but for all products, please make sure to first read the directions and recommended safety precautions. You should consider adding a respirator, safety glasses, and gloves to your cosplay toolbox. Your future self will thank you! With that out of the way, here is a list of entry-level tools for working with EVA foam:

CUTTING AND MEASURING TOOLS

Similar to the tools for sewing, you'll want a few options for working with foam, including utility knives, precision blades, scissors (not your fabric pair!), and more utilitarian rulers, to be used with said sharp implements.

A newer addition to crafting is a cutting machine, which can be used to cut and add details to thinner sheets of EVA foam.

SANDPAPER AND ROTARY TOOL

Using sandpaper or a rotary tool, you can clean up and smooth your edges, create bevels, and even carve in details. When using a power tool, keep in mind those safety tips mentioned earlier, and always test on a scrap piece of foam before trying on your freshly cut one.

HEAT GUN

Likely the most important tool you'll use while working with EVA foam is a heat gun. Once heated, the foam will soften, allowing you to manipulate it into the shape you want. Heat guns also help you prepare the foam for priming and painting in a process called heat sealing. Heat guns are typically affordable and accessible, but in a pinch, a hair dryer is a good substitute. Remember to keep your work setup in mind, as heat guns are designed to get hot, which can melt tables or even cause a fire.

ADHESIVES

It's gluing time! There are a wide variety of adhesives out there, which have differing levels of bond strength. Not all are good for permanent use, like spray adhesives and tape. But there is a collection of ones that do the job well: contact cement, quick-cure, and hot glue. When deciding which ones to use, you'll want to consider what project you're working on, bond time and strength, and the toxicity of the glue. And make sure to read those warning labels and wear your respirator when needed.

A cutting tool, heat gun, and sandpaper are essential to your cosplay toolkit.

ADDITIONAL THERMOPLASTICS FOR COSPLAY

Although EVA foam has become the standard in cosplay circles, there are a few other options, such as Worbla. Also a thermoplastic, Worbla has a more rigid shape than EVA foam, and can be used with foam to add details or shore up a form. As it can be a little pricier, most use Worbla for smaller jobs or to finish a piece. There are some incredible tutorials online showing how to use Worbla and foam together, plus things to do with the scrap pieces.

INTRODUCTION TO 3D PRINTING

The last skill I'll talk about is also the newest addition to the cosplay community: 3D printing. Though the technology to 3D print has been around for more than forty years, it has only become more accessible in the last five years or so. Again, I promise to not get into the scientific details, but the technology and materials have advanced to a point where an entry-level printer can be purchased for less than $200. And it's even compact enough to fit in a New York City apartment.

Though this skill can certainly require more of a learning curve, it's not necessary to purchase one to add a 3D-printed element to your cosplay. Just as you can commission the fabric pieces of a costume, you

Sam of Black Zero Cosplay blends foam and fabric to bring his Doctor Doom to life.

can purchase a premade 3D-printed object, or even a file to be used on a friend's printer. That is basically what I do when I need something printed. Currently, it can be costly to print a larger object, but 3D printing is a great solution for smaller props and costume accessories like belt buckles or arc reactors.

★ ★ THE FINISHING TOUCHES ★ ★

WITH BOTH EVA FOAM AND 3D PRINTING, YOU'LL WANT to make sure to add time for finishing: priming, painting, and deciding how to assemble the pieces for your costume. Priming for each can be a little different, but the basic idea is to seal in the shape and prepare the surface for painting. Every cosplayer has their own preferred product, with several options out there for you to choose from.

When you're ready to paint, there are many tools and techniques to learn, most of which require trial and error, a little patience, and more room than I have in this book. In Beverly Downen's book, *Cosplayer's*

Marvel's host Lorraine Cink in her Scarlet Witch cosplay created for *Marvel Method*.

Ultimate Guide to EVA Foam, her priming and painting chapter is twenty-six pages! I'll leave it to our cosplayers to break down their preferred processes for working with and finishing both EVA foam and 3D prints.

The greatest thing about cosplay is the community. This might be a theme I repeat again and again in this book, but it really is true. It's incredible how many cosplayers are willing to share their experiences making costumes, including personal tips and tricks.

It only takes a quick search online to find tutorials and drafted patterns. Going back to the days of forums, like cosplay.com and the Replica Prop Forum, there has always been a space for costumers and cosplayers to share and learn new skills. Accessibility has expanded even more with social media and online videos. No matter how big the community grows, the most important thing is to remember that there is always room for more.

And as you tackle each new skill, there are a few things to keep in mind. First, don't forget that cosplay is hard. We all had to begin from somewhere, so don't feel let down if the first attempt isn't perfect or you have a hiccup when you're painting. Sometimes those little mistakes end up teaching you a new technique or even end up creating a better look. Second, there is really no ceiling to the cosplay you'd like to do. Remember those costumes you see on screen (even those created in special effects) have a human being—or many—making them. Really, the lesson is, don't limit yourself, and always be open to learning something new.

Now to celebrate the expansiveness of the Marvel cosplay community, I've invited six cosplayers to share their processes of creating costumes, from Captain America's suit, Loki's helm, and Jean Grey's wig. Join them as they walk you through the materials and steps to assembling each cosplay!

Marvel Cosplay Online—
Marvel Becoming and More!

★ ★ ★

As social media grew from forums to photos and then videos, it was natural Marvel would follow right along, finding new ways to feature cosplay. Here are just a few of the moments.

Launched in 2011, Costoberfest was a monthly celebration of cosplay and costuming across Marvel's social channels, starting with Facebook and Tumblr, and expanding to Twitter, Instagram, and Marvel.com over the years. Every October, from 2011 to 2019, we'd highlight a different cosplayer or group, with fans submitting photos from almost every continent and countless countries. It was always an incredible joy to open the inbox and see what new photos we received!

Judy with Yaya Han on set for the first season of *Marvel Becoming*.

With each year, the awareness of cosplay continued to expand, not only in the industry but also internally, enough so that in 2014, I was able to pitch my first cosplay video series: *Marvel Method*. Born from an office discussion on how cosplay is really created, we welcomed professional costumer (and friend) Carly Bradt to help us build a Scarlet Witch costume for host Lorraine Cink to wear. Over five episodes, the series walked fans through choosing fabrics, making a pattern, sewing, and final accessories. The final episode follows Lorraine as she debuts the cosplay at SDCC.

From those early roots, the beginnings of *Marvel Becoming* began to grow. In 2016, I was given a budget of $3,600 and charged with producing twelve short videos highlighting cosplay. As mentioned in chapter 1, those early episodes were accomplished thanks to friends, who became guinea pigs as I discovered what this series could be. Enter my soon-to-be director, Jason Latorre.

With Jason by my side, we launched the first season to much success, and we go on to push ourselves each year. The second season focused on stunning cosplay shots and interviews. We next introduced making-of and convention moments in the following seasons, all leading up to our cosplayers' experience at the giant Marvel gathering at Dragon Con.

Over seventy episodes, we set out to have *Marvel Becoming* highlight the complexity of the cosplay community: color, age, size, skill level, and origin story. Across my fifteen-year career, some of my favorite moments are the phone calls asking our cosplayers if they'd like to join us on *Becoming*. Each conversation would end with tears of joy, excited shouts, and a fan's dream come true.

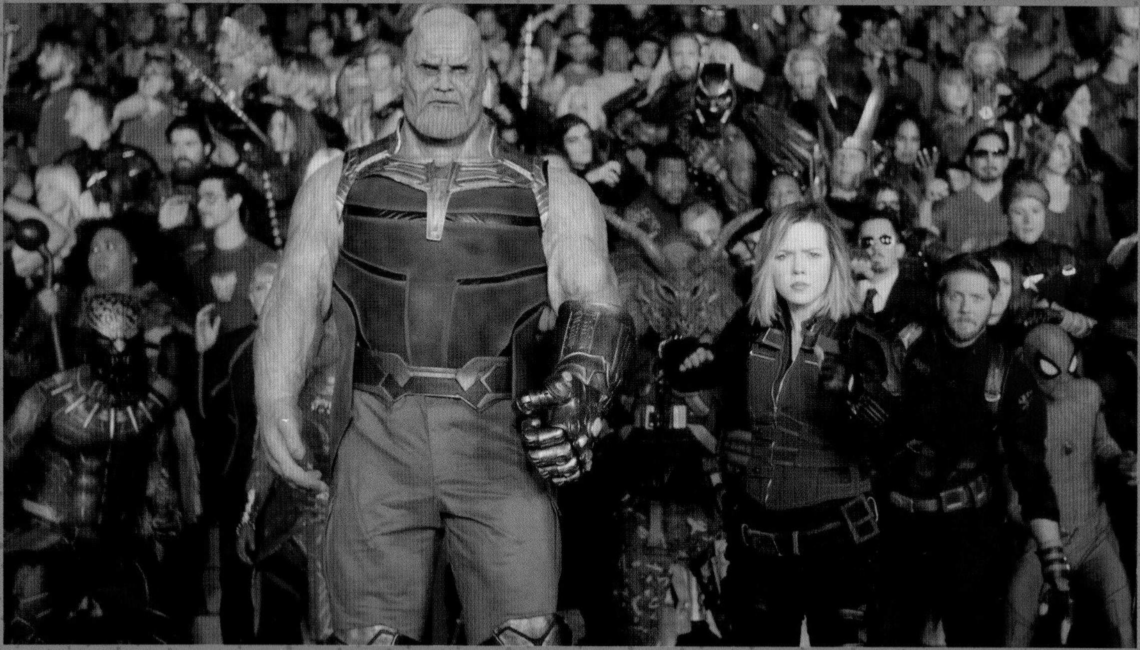

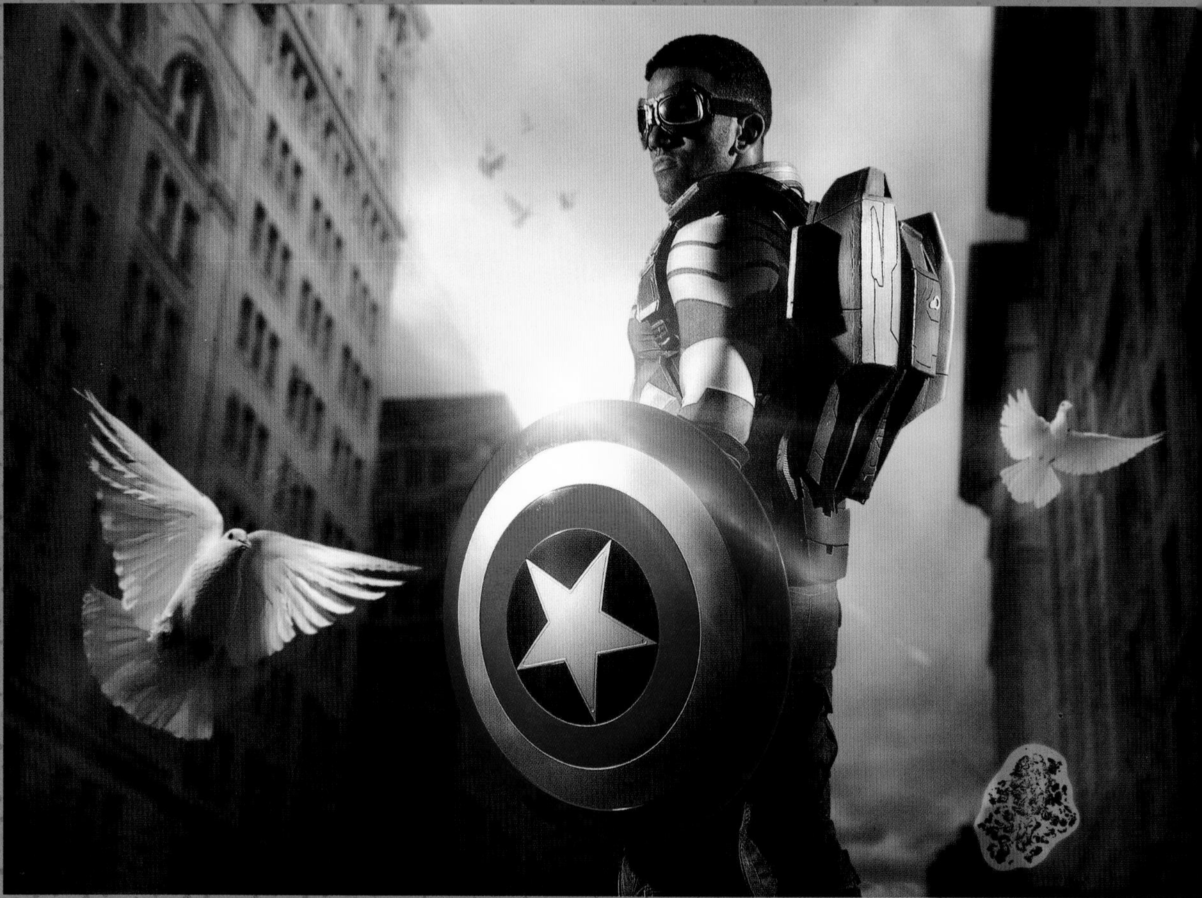

TOP LEFT: At Atlanta's Dragon Con, HurleyFX and Romanovarose dressed as Thanos and Black Widow.

BOTTOM LEFT: Blerd Vision's Sam Wilson in New York.

TOP RIGHT: Titan Cosplay's Planet Hulk behind the scenes in Texas.

BOTTOM RIGHT: Three Captain Marvels—Pitchfork Cosplay, Sharon Rose, and CutiePieSensei.

PART II

BECOMING A MARVEL COSPLAYER

★ ★ ★

CHAPTER 4

The Marvelous Ms. Marvel

★ ★ One of Marvel's Newest Heroes: Ms. Marvel ★ ★

"Embiggen!"

Being a fan of comics in the twenty-first century means you're able to meet new heroes, and sometimes that hero may actually look like you. For many South Asian fans, that experience happened when Marvel announced that a new hero, a Pakistani American teenage girl, Kamala Khan, would become the next Ms. Marvel. Now, ten years later, she has been fully integrated into the league of Earth's Mightiest Heroes.

BEFORE SHE DISCOVERED HER POWERS, KAMALA WAS like the rest of us, a fan of the super heroes in her comics—though in her world, those heroes were real, with actual superpowers. Growing up in New Jersey, with the skyline of New York City visible just over the river, she spent her days and nights dreaming of meeting her idols, like Captain Marvel. But her life would be changed forever, when the Inhumans' Terrigen Mist was released into the Earth's atmosphere, waking her latent Inhuman abilities, and empowering her to alter shape and size.

Prior to her transformation, the Muslim American youth had worked through the typical teenage problems, like struggling to fit in at school, while balancing her family's religious and spiritual beliefs with the society she lived in. Now with the opportunity to aid her community with her new powers, Kamala quickly crafted her own costume identity and adopted the Ms. Marvel mantle.

It had only been a few years since Carol Danvers had sunset the name, stepping into her new era with the legacy title Captain Marvel. Since her first super hero fight in *Ms. Marvel #1* in 1977, Carol had

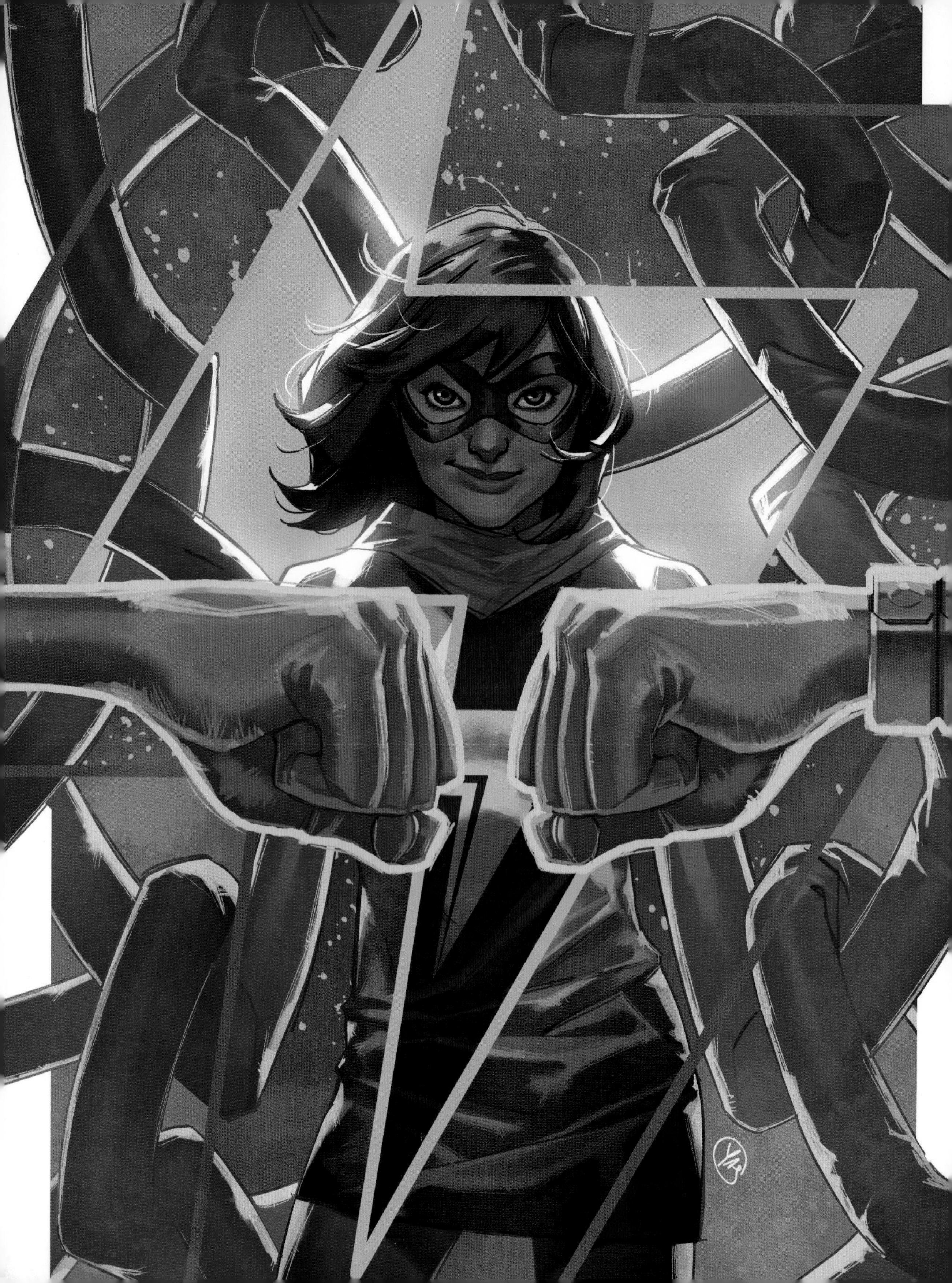

stood alongside the Avengers, protecting not only Earth but alien worlds near and far. And Kamala's co-creators, Sana Amanat and G. Willow Wilson, drew from that history while bringing a fresh, youthful take to a new hero. And like her idol before her, Kamala would find her own way, with the support of her friends and family, and become a new kind of hero. Even now, Ms. Marvel continues to remind us all that being a hero is more than punching the bad guys; it's really about helping those who need it.

★ ★ RAISA KARIM, @RAISINCOSPLAY ★ ★

HALLOWEEN HAS BEEN A CLEAR ENTRY POINT for many cosplayers, including Raisa Karim, our Ms. Marvel cosplayer. Born and raised in Florida, but now a New Yorker, Raisa discovered cosplay about ten years ago in 2013. "I have always loved Halloween, and one year I wanted to make a Batgirl costume, so I started researching super hero costumes. I came across the word 'cosplay' and discovered icons like Yaya Han and Kamui Cosplay. Then my dad took me to my first con and that was that!"

From there it was easy enough for her to fall deeper into cosplay, as sewing had been a part of her life for as long as she could remember, thanks to a friend of her mother's who taught her how to sew. With a few costumes under her belt, Raisa's first Marvel cosplay was a gender-swapped Wiccan, from Jamie McKelvie and Kieron Gillen's run of the *Young Avengers*. After she posted it on Tumblr, Jamie actually reblogged it!

It was through cosplay that she found one of the rare spaces where she could feel wholly accepted. After growing up feeling like an outsider, within the cosplay community she found acceptance and great friends. "You are never treated like an outsider. People that are neurodivergent, introverted, or have fringe interests blossom in this community. There's nobody too weird or too awkward for us!"

41

Raisa poses in her Ms. Marvel cosplay, built using a mix of sewn and prepurchased items.

"One of the best parts of cosplaying at a convention is sharing rooms with other cosplayers. Need to fix your costume last minute? They'll help. Forgot to bring a hot glue gun? Someone's definitely got one."

—Raisa Karim

From creating clothes for her stuffed animals to immaculate costumes, Raisa continues to push herself and her skills. Recently she has fallen in love with 3D modeling. "I feel that all of these skills are connected. Sewing and patternmaking are about turning 2D concepts into 3D shapes, and the same is true for EVA foam armor and 3D modeling." With her patternmaking and draping skills, she creates foam armor patterns that are available online. She continues, "In my opinion, the key to building skills is not to jump into strange territory, but rather to explore new areas connected to the skills you already have."

Just like Kamala, Raisa is a South Asian Desi Muslim who has been obsessed with super heroes her whole life. "I never grew up with representations of myself, so when Marvel made a super hero who was a brown Muslim girl, it blew me away. There have been many legacy characters created for diversity, but they never truly lasted. Kamala did, and she grew up with me."

With the experience she has built throughout her time as a cosplayer, Raisa will walk you through how she made the very first iteration of Kamala's Ms. Marvel costume, Adrian Alphona's design from *Ms. Marvel Vol. 1: No Normal*.

MAKING OF
★ ★ KAMALA KHAN AKA MS. MARVEL ★ ★

COSPLAY BUILD NOTES

FOR OUR FIRST BUILD, WE WILL INTRODUCE YOU TO three of the main techniques you'll use in cosplay: patterning, sewing, and appliqué. You'll be crafting two pieces of Ms. Marvel's costume, the tunic and scarf, while adding details to purchased items (Kamala's mask, gauntlets, and boots). To keep the build simple, we'll also be using a purchased red t-shirt with forearm-length sleeves and matching leggings for her undersuit. For the tunic, we'll be using an already owned well-fitting dress as a template to make the pattern and introducing you to a few of the options for appliqué to add on the iconic lightning bolt.

Finally, when looking for a wig, either online or in store, aim for a color brown that matches your complexion and head shape. Length and style is up to you, but we used a medium-length wavy wig with bangs.

MATERIALS

TUNIC AND SCARF

- 1 to 2 yards of royal blue stretch knit fabric, such as spandex or jersey
- 1 yard of gold metallic stretch vinyl fabric
- Gold iron-on vinyl (heat transfer vinyl, or HTV) for stretch fabrics (optional)
- 1 to 2 yards of red lightweight fabric, such as chiffon
- Blue, red, and gold thread
- 18- to 22-inch blue zipper, length dependent on size of tunic
- Shoulder pads

PURCHASED ACCESSORIES

- Mask
- Fitted dress for pattern mockup

- Wavy brown wig with bangs
- Red t-shirt with forearm-length sleeves
- Red leggings
- Gold cuffs
- Blue boots

ADDITIONAL SEWING AND CRAFTING ITEMS

- Pattern paper
- Chalk or fabric marker
- Craft knife
- Iron, ironing board, and pressing cloth
- Pins
- Ruler
- Scissors
- Sewing machine with zipper foot
- Vinyl cutter (optional)

STEP-BY-STEP GUIDE

BUILDING THE TUNIC PATTERN

1. Lay the fitted dress down on your pattern paper and secure it with pins or weights.

2. Trace the shape of the dress onto the pattern paper. Depending on the stretch of the item you're using, adjust the width along the sides. To assist later in matching corresponding edges, add in notches on each seam.

3. Cut out the shape and label. This will be the pattern piece for the front.

4. To add in the zipper for the back, copy the existing pattern onto a second piece of paper.

5. Draw a vertical line down the center from the collar to the bottom hem. Add in ½-inch seam allowance on one side, and mark where the zipper will end, roughly 18 inches down from the collar.

6. Cut out and label the modified back pattern pieces, marking the left and right sides accordingly.

7. Next, laying the blue fashion fabric right side down, transfer your patterns to the fabric using chalk or a marker.

8. Cut out the front and two back pieces.

9. When finished, you should have the following pattern pieces: 1 front and 2 back.

SEWING THE TUNIC

1. Start by taking the front and the left back piece and match the right sides of the fabric together.
2. Pin along the side seams, making sure to match the notches.
3. Stitch from the underarm to the bottom of the tunic.
4. Then repeat for the right back piece.
   Now, we will add the gold trim to each of the raw edges of the tunic.
5. Start by measuring the lengths of the bottom hem, neckline, and armhole. Record the measurements.
6. Measure out the recorded lengths of your gold vinyl fabric, then mark 2½-inch-wide strips on the back side.
7. Cut out the 2½-inch-wide pieces of gold fabric.
8. Fold the gold fabric at the center, with wrong sides together, and baste it together at the edges.
9. Pin each trim piece to its corresponding hem, neckline, and armhole edges, and then sew together.
10. Last, fold the edge of the trim under, pinning it to the wrong side of the fabric, and topstitch with a narrow zigzag.

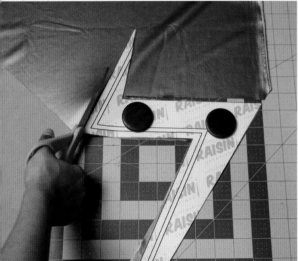

ADDING THE LIGHTNING BOLT EMBLEM

Before finishing the tunic, we will add Ms. Marvel's emblem. You'll need one lightning bolt, created either by hand or using a computer program. Once ready, you can apply the emblem one of two ways:

OPTION 1:
IRON-ON HEAT-TRANSFER VINYL (HTV)

1. Using iron-on vinyl, cut out the template by hand using a craft knife, or with a vinyl cutting machine. Be sure you have flipped the template and are cutting on the side of the vinyl that does not have the glossy plastic over it.
2. With pins or chalk, mark on the fabric where you'd like to position your lightning bolt.
3. Lay down the emblem, cover with a pressing cloth, and then iron on the vinyl according to the instructions.
4. Once cooled down, peel away the protective plastic to reveal the final emblem.

OPTION 2:
FABRIC APPLIQUÉ

1. Using the same gold fabric as your trim, mark out the lightning bolt using your template, then cut it out with your sharpest fabric scissors.
2. With pins or chalk, mark on the fabric where you'd like to position your emblem.
3. With an adhesive tool, such as spray basting or iron-on adhesive, secure the emblem to the tunic.
4. With matching gold thread, sew a narrow straight or zigzag stitch all along the edge of the appliqué.

TIP: Depending on what material you're using, you'll want to iron any wrinkles out of your fabric as you build your pattern.

FINISHING THE TUNIC

1. Starting on the right side of the tunic, pin and sew the tops of both shoulder seams closed.
2. Next, you'll install the zipper. Pin the zipper to the inside (wrong side of fabric) back left side of the tunic and then, using your zipper foot, stitch it onto the fabric. Repeat with the other side of the zipper.
3. Then, you'll create the shoulder pieces. Draw out the shape of your shoulder pads on the blue fashion fabric, adding a 2-inch seam allowance all around, with additional allowance at the edge to attach it to the tunic.
4. Pulling fabric tight to retain the shape and baste along the edge.
5. Hand sew the pads into the shoulder seam allowance of the tunic.

TIP: When sewing a zipper to a stretch material, there are a few ways you can prevent any misalignment or buckling, like using hand stitching or basting the zipper down first.

FINAL ACCESSORIES

The accessories are where you can go simple or big in your cosplay. Do what works for you!

1. For your scarf: measure and cut out a long, skinny rectangle of your red fashion fabric—it should be long enough to wrap around your neck and hang down your back. Finish the edges with a simple hem, such as a rolled hem.
2. For your gauntlets: use purchased gold cuffs or create them using EVA foam (see chapter 7 to learn more!). Just remember to think about how you'll pull the gauntlet on and off.
3. For your boots: use a purchased pair of blue boots or use blue paint or leftover blue fabric to cover a pair you own. Same for the mask!

TIP: You can attach the mask to your face without elastic using a prosthetic adhesive such as spirit gum or Pros-Aide!

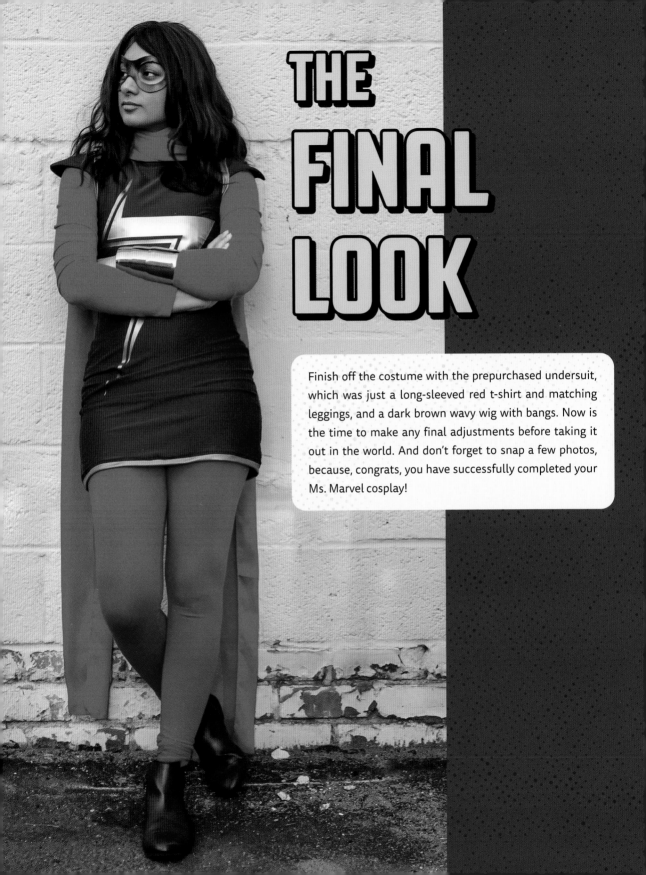

THE FINAL LOOK

Finish off the costume with the prepurchased undersuit, which was just a long-sleeved red t-shirt and matching leggings, and a dark brown wavy wig with bangs. Now is the time to make any final adjustments before taking it out in the world. And don't forget to snap a few photos, because, congrats, you have successfully completed your Ms. Marvel cosplay!

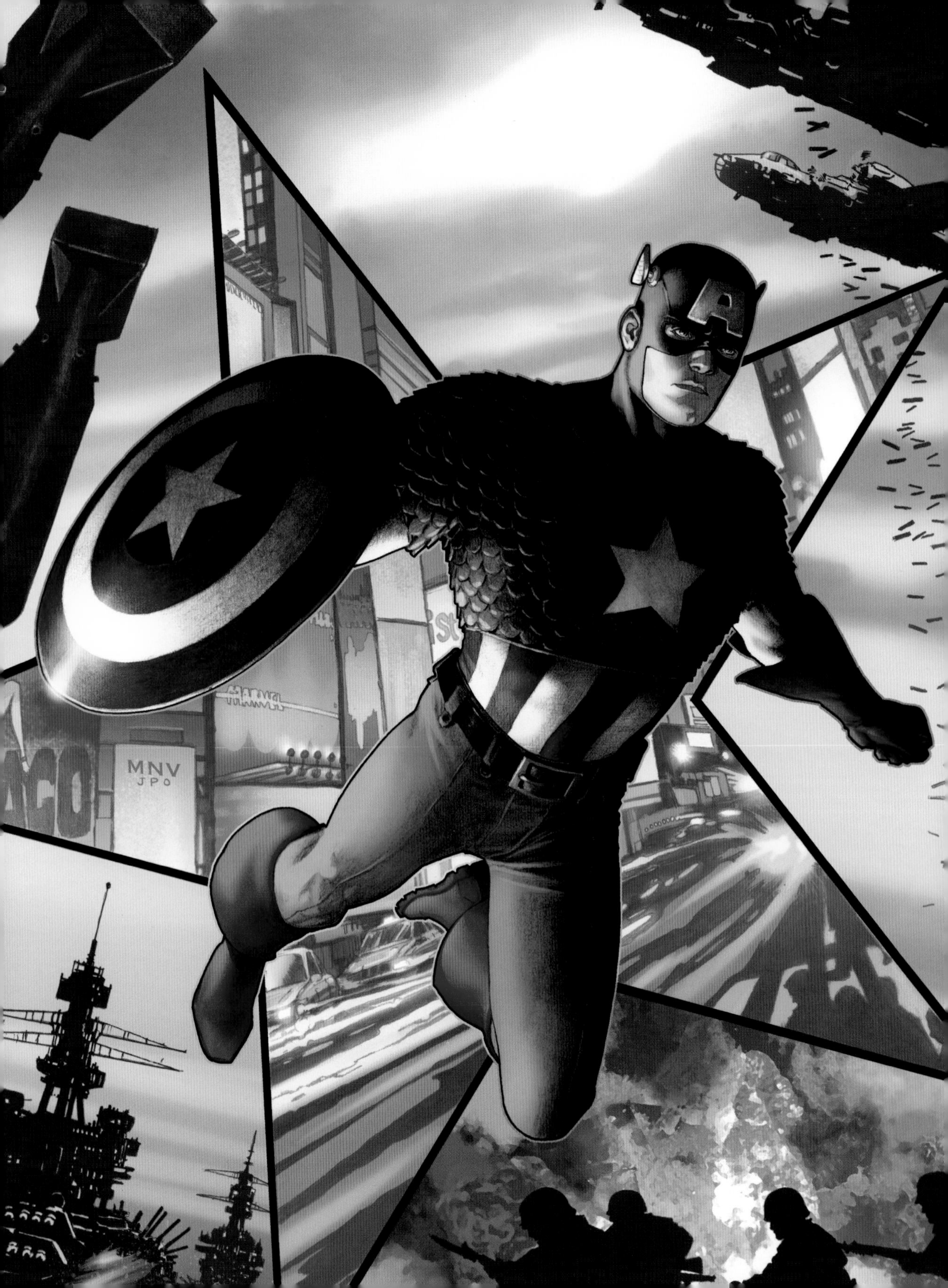
MARVEL
MNV
JPO

The Sentinel of Liberty—Captain America

★ ★ The Story of the Iconic Captain America ★ ★

"Avengers, ASSEMBLE!"

Ever since Captain America was splashed across the cover of *Captain America #1* in 1941, he has been an icon—a sentinel of liberty—to shield the oppressed and fight for freedom everywhere. And now more than eighty years later, Steve and his shield, co-created by Joe Simon and Jack Kirby, still very much matter to current generations and make him an easy choice for many first-time cosplayers. And it is thanks to the Marvel Studios films that there now have been so many new fans introduced to Steve and his many suits from comics to games to the big screen. So, who is the *first* Avenger?

FIRST, WE HAVE TO GO BACK IN TIME TO THE DAYS leading up to the United States preparing to join the Allied powers in World War II. A poor Brooklyn orphan, Steve Rogers looked to do his duty, enlisting in the army, but was rejected due to his small size and under-developed physique. Even stuck in those unhappy cir-cumstances, he truly believed he was more than just a "ninety-eight-pound weakling." And so did Professor Abraham Erskine, a pioneer in the development of the super-soldier project. Seeing Steve's potential, Erskine inducted him into Project Rebirth, where the super-serum enhanced Steve's frail body, transform-ing it to a new tall and muscular one with amazing strength and agility.

Now armed with his new powers and a nearly indestructible shield, Steve would go on to be a World War II hero, on the front lines and at home. But he would not see the Allied powers win the war. During a fight with the Red Skull, after an experimental plane was brought down, Steve and his shield were lost to time in the ice.

Decades later, his future super hero team, the Avengers, would awaken him from his sleep into a modern world. And even as a man out of time, Steve gladly reclaimed the Captain America shield, became the leader of the Avengers, and continued to fight for his American ideals. From protecting his home against villainous assaults to stopping alien invasions, Steve has been right there at the front line.

Through the years, others have become Captain America when Steve couldn't, including two of his allies. After the events of *Civil War*, with Steve assumed dead, his childhood friend and fellow World War II veteran, James Buchanan "Bucky" Barnes, would take up the mantle for a time. Then, later on, when Steve was drained of his powers by the villainous Iron Nail, he looked to a friend and fellow Avenger, Sam Wilson, the Falcon, to take over as the next Captain America.

Throughout the years, no matter who dons the red, white, and blue, Captain America is always one of the world's mightiest heroes—the sentinel of liberty, far beyond the borders of the United States, with the iconic shield transcending race, sex, and age. Say it with me, "Avengers, assemble!"

MEET THE COSPLAYER:

★ ★ MARK MATTHEWS, @SCRAPPERCOSTUMING ★ ★

NO BETTER PLACE TO START COSPLAYING A MARVEL character than with the original Avenger, Captain America. It was almost natural for Mark Matthews to follow with five more versions of Steve Rogers, from the comics to the silver screen. Based just a few miles north up the Hudson River in Rockland County, Mark says his origin story leads back to homemade costumes and early sewing skills taught to him by his mother and grandmother. It was in high school that he first learned about cosplay as an anime fan. But it wasn't until college, in 2015, after finding himself in a new community with like-minded individuals who just happened to cosplay, that he finally decided to jump in.

"I remember finding out my friend was building an Iron Man Mk III suit in his dorm room. This was around the time *Age of Ultron* was released, so it was the prime time to start on my first Captain America suit, which has become a staple of my cosplay wardrobe."

With those family sewing lessons as groundwork, Mark has continued to build on his skills, including learning 3D modeling in college. Now with almost ten years of cosplay under his belt, along with a community of friends who are willing to share knowledge and collaborate, he has amassed a wide collection of Marvel costumes, from Captain America, Spider-Man, and Loki to Iron Man armor. He's also working on a Classic Loki from the Disney+ series, and another Captain America, this time from the *Ultimates* comics.

"I think I love Steve Rogers for a lot of the same reasons that I love Peter Parker. While they're very different characters, they both have similar, strong convictions to do the right thing—no matter what the personal cost will be, no matter who is or isn't watching. I think Cap is one of those magical characters who really embodies the core, boiled-down concept of what it means to be a hero in that way. His fight has cost him so much over the years, but he keeps getting up and continuing to take the punches, because he can and it's the right thing to do. I think there's a real nobility to that."

With as many suits as Mark has made, he's not previously had the opportunity to go back in time, to recreate the classic 1960s Jack Kirby design. So he was eager to jump right into the project, with "his bright, punchy colors, the big star across the chest, and the buccaneer style boots, it's very over the top and larger than life." From the 2D comic page to a fully fleshed out costume, join Mark as he walks you through the steps for creating your very own Captain America.

THE MAKING OF

★ ★ STEVE ROGERS, AKA CAPTAIN AMERICA ★ ★

COSPLAY BUILD NOTES

FOR OUR NEXT PROJECT, WE WILL CONTINUE TO BUILD and expand our skills in our three main techniques: patterning, sewing, and appliqué. You'll be crafting four pieces for Steve's 1960s suit: the base striped top, the scaled top piece, pants, and a set of briefs. Depending on your preferences, you can make adjustments as needed for your costume, such as skipping making the briefs or combining the two top pieces into one garment. With this build, we are using a printed fabric that resembles scales, but if you're unable to source a similar fabric, you can just as easily use the same blue fabric you're using for the pants to make a great-looking Captain America suit.

For our patterns, we'll be using pre-assembled spandex bodysuits to draft out the different pieces of the suit. You can also sew your own test suit, using scrap spandex material. For the cowl and accessories like the gloves and shield, you can either purchase them via a Marvel licensee or cosplay commissioner, look online for patterns to make your own, or mix and match, depending on your timeline and budget.

Mark poses in one of his many cosplays of Captain America.

"My grandfather was a man of smaller stature who joined the army. Though he wasn't able to take a Super-Soldier Serum, he was able to use his exceptional mind for math to serve his country to the best of his ability, eventually becoming a captain."

—Mark Matthews

MATERIALS

SUPER SUIT (TOP, PANTS, AND BRIEFS)
- Spandex bodysuit
- 2 yards of white spandex
- 1 yard of red spandex
- 2 to 3 yards of blue spandex
- ½ yard of white canvas, or similar white fabric
- Blue and white thread
- 3 yards of ½-inch elastic

PURCHASED ACCESSORIES
- Captain America shield
- Cowl or helmet

- Black belt
- Red buccaneer boots
- Red gauntlet gloves

ADDITIONAL SEWING AND CRAFTING ITEMS
- Chalk or fabric marker
- Iron, ironing board, and pressing cloth
- Pattern paper
- Pins
- Ruler
- Scissors
- Sewing machine

STEP-BY-STEP GUIDE

BUILDING THE SUPER SUIT PATTERN

To create a pattern for each of the pieces, you will start with a purchased spandex bodysuit with the hands, feet, and hood removed.

1. Start by drawing a symmetrical line down the front and back of the bodysuit to assist later when mirroring the patterns.
2. Then, once you are wearing the bodysuit, either asking a favor from a friend, or by yourself in front of a mirror, mark out the following main elements:

FRONT TOP PIECE:

Start by drawing a horizontal line just under your bust from your left underarm to your right. This pattern piece will be used for both your front and back.

SLEEVE:

There are multiple ways to draft a sleeve. For this build, we connected the sleeve lines to the collar. Start by drawing a diagonal line from the collar to your underarm, at the center point of your side. Then, for the arm seam, you'll draw a straight line from the underside of your wrist to your underarm. This will be used for both your left and right arms. For the shortened blue sleeves, start by marking a horizontal line at the center of your biceps. This should loosely match up with your bust line for the top.

TIP: Unless you have extra fabric, it is always a good idea to plan out how each pattern will fit on the fabric, taking stretch and bias into consideration. If any of your fabrics have directional patterns on them, make sure your patterns sit in a way so that the patterns will go in the correct direction and match up when the garments are assembled.

ABDOMINAL STRIPES:

Start by measuring and marking out 16 abdominal vertical stripes: 8 white and 8 red. (For a 40-inch bust and 36-inch waist, the red stripes are 2 inches wide, and the white are 2¼ inches wide.)

TIP: For patterns like these red and white stripes, you can also use fabric paint to create them, or even look to find a printed spandex material at your local fabric store that matches!

FRONT AND BACK LEG:

Start by drawing two lines down your leg. The first will be the outside seam, running from your waist down your hip to your ankle. The second will be drawn along the inside of your leg, from the center point of your crotch to the ankle. These two seams should be parallel going down your leg. If adding briefs, mark the shape, including the length of the legs.

TIP: It may seem tedious to clearly label and mark each pattern piece and corresponding fabric pieces. But you'll learn that this will guide you as you cut out and begin to build the suit.

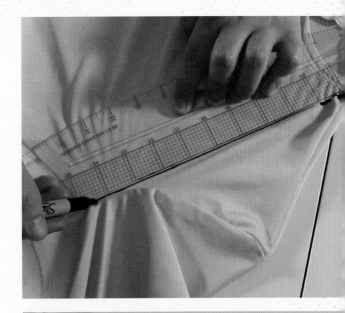

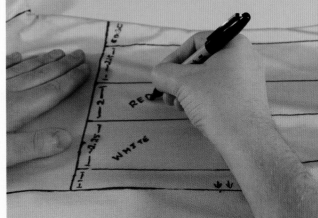

1. Remove the bodysuit and then clean up the drafted marks, making sure to properly label and identify each piece.
2. Cut out each pattern piece. Remember: since you'll be mirroring patterns, you only need to cut out one leg and one sleeve pattern, as well as one white and one red stripe.
3. When finished, you should have the following pattern pieces: 1 top front and back, 1 sleeve, 1 red stripe, 1 white stripe, 1 front leg (with notes for briefs), 1 back leg (with notes for briefs).
4. Next, transfer each piece onto pattern paper, smoothing out any rough lines or curves.
5. With a ruler, add ½-inch seam allowance for each piece. For your pants and briefs, add 4½ inches to the top of your waist edge for the elastic band.
6. Add and copy any final notes and notches on your patterns, then cut out each pattern piece.
7. Lay each pattern down on the corresponding fabric, wrong side up, and mark out the following pieces:

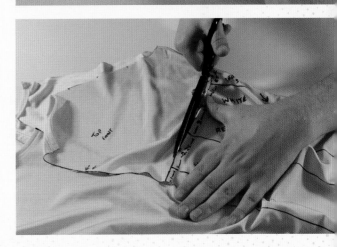

WHITE SPANDEX:

- 2 top pieces, front/back
- 2 sleeves
- 8 stripes

RED SPANDEX:

- 8 stripes

TIP: Depending on your pattern, you may also want to add additional length at the waist or other points to help when assembling later on.

BLUE SPANDEX:

- 2 tops, front/back
- 2 short sleeves
- 2 front legs
- 2 back legs
- 2 front briefs
- 2 back briefs

Transfer any lines and notches onto the fabric, then cut out all your pieces.

SEWING THE "STRIPE" SHIRT

1. Starting with a red stripe in the middle, pin and then stitch together your stripes in an alternating red and white pattern for both the front and back of your shirt.
2. To attach to the top of the shirt, align the top edge of the front stripe panel to the bottom edge of the shirt front, pin and sew. Then repeat with the back.

TIP: When using stretch fabric, aim to use a zigzag stitch, as it will be easier to manage, plus creates more secure seams.

3. To attach the sleeves, starting with the left sleeve, with right sides of fabric facing, align the front shoulder edge to the corresponding edge on the front pattern. Pin and then sew.
4. Repeat this process for the back of the sleeve and top seam.
5. Repeat steps 3 and 4 for the right sleeve.
6. To finish the shirt, start at the wrist of the left sleeve and sew the bottom seam, going up to the underarm, and then turning to follow down the side to end at the waist. Repeat for the right sleeve.

TIP: Anytime you have to lift the presser foot to change the direction of the seam, always remember to keep the needle in the fabric as you pivot it to prevent any shifting.

7. Turn the shirt right side out and check the fit. Then finish any unfinished edges to your liking.

ADDING THE STAR EMBLEM

Before stitching together the scale top, we're going to add Captain America's iconic stars to your "scale" or blue fabric. You'll need two stars: a small star for the front of the suit and a larger star for the back.

1. Start by measuring and then drawing a 7-inch and an 8-inch star for your template, either by hand or using a digital template. Depending on the size of your top, you can adjust the dimension of the star to be larger or smaller for the best fit.

2. Trace your templated stars onto your white canvas fabric, and then cut out each star.

3. With pins or chalk, mark on the fabric where you'd like to position your stars.

4. With an adhesive tool, such as spray basting or iron-on adhesive, secure the star to the top.

5. Do the same on the back with the larger star.

6. Topstitch along the edges of the star to secure it. If you would like to further finish the edge and add some detail, sew a second pass around each star with a zigzag stitch.

SEWING THE "SCALE" (OR BLUE) SHIRT

1. Repeat steps 3 through 6 from the striped shirt to sew the front, back, and sleeve panels into a single piece.

2. Turn the shirt right side out and check the fit. Then finish any unfinished edges to your liking.

SEWING THE PANTS AND BRIEFS

1. Starting with the right sides of the front and back leg patterns, align the outside edges, then pin and sew. Repeat this step for the other leg.

2. Next, connect the right and left sides of your pants together by pinning then sewing along the front and back vertical center seams.

3. To finish, starting with the right ankle, pin and then sew along the inside leg seam (right ankle to the crotch and down to the left ankle).

4. Turn the pants right side out and check the fit. Then finish the bottom hems as desired.

TIP: When sewing high-stress areas like the crotch of the pants, you may want to pass over the area a second, or even third, time with your machine to ensure your seam is secure and prevent any costume malfunctions.

5. Repeat steps 1 through 4 for the briefs. Next, you'll add the elastic to the pants and briefs.

6. Using your waist measurement, cut the length of elastic to that length plus a few inches at each end for overlap and stretch.

7. Take your elastic and line it up with the waistband, starting just beyond the back center seam, then pin.

8. Using a ¾-inch seam allowance and a zigzag stitch, sew along the edge. When you finish going around the waist, the elastic should overlap a small amount at the back center seam.

9. Fold the elastic down onto the inside of the pants, until the fabric fully covers the elastic.

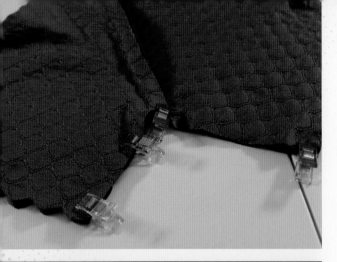

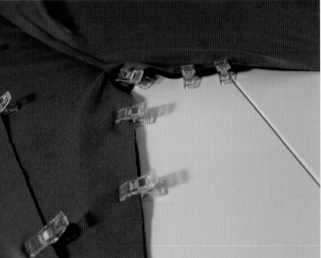

10. Repeat the process of sewing around the waist, holding the elastic at its natural tautness. To make sure the elastic is hidden, use a 1-inch seam allowance.

TIP: When sewing with elastic, you want to pull the elastic slightly taut, keeping the tension as consistent as possible.

11. Repeat steps 6 through 10 to add elastic to the waist of the briefs.

    Last, you'll add belt loops to the briefs. If you did not make the briefs, then add the loops to your pants.

12. Start by measuring out five rectangles that are 3 inches wide, with the length twice the width of your belt, plus a 1-inch seam allowance on each side. Cut these out of blue spandex. (For example, my belt is ½-inch wide, so the measurement would be 3 inches by 3 inches.)

13. To create the loop, fold the rectangle in half horizontally, matching the right sides together, pin, and sew along the longer edges. Repeat for all five loops.

14. Turn each right side out and iron them flat.

15. Sew the short unfinished edges together on each tube to make a loop, and iron again in the same way to make the belt loops nice and crisp.

16. Before attaching, using chalk or pins, mark the location on the briefs' waist for each loop, starting at the center back seam, then measure out where the other four will sit.

17. Pin each loop and double-check the placement.

18. Finally, using either your sewing machine or a hand stitch, sew each loop onto your briefs.

THE FINAL LOOK

With your top, pants, and briefs built, you're almost ready to charge into battle. Finish off the costume with pre-purchased gauntlets, red gauntlet gloves, buccaneer boots, and a black belt. Take a look to make any final adjustments, then it's time to pick up the iconic shield, and assemble the Avengers, in your very own Captain America cosplay!

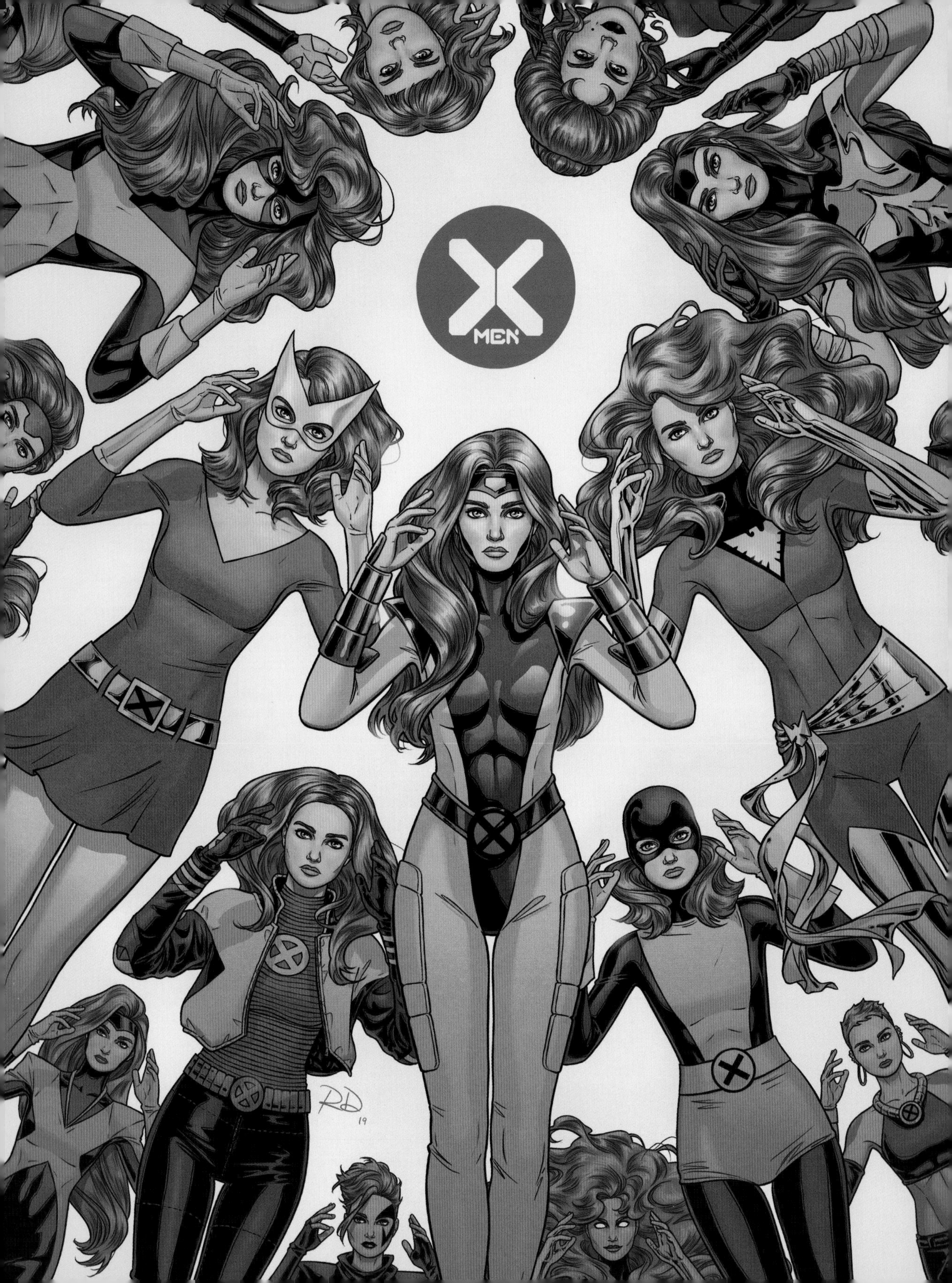
X
MEN

CHAPTER 6

A Founding Member of the X-Men— Jean Grey

★ ★ More Than Just the Phoenix ★ ★

"I am fire and life incarnate!
Now and forever—I am Phoenix!"

FROM THE BEGINNING, THE X-MEN HAVE ALWAYS BEEN a little bit different from the rest of the Marvel super heroes. Gifted—or, for some, cursed—with extra unusual abilities and appearances, these mutants have still aimed to protect the world that hates and fears them. Going back to their origins in the 1960s, and throughout the years, the X-Men have represented a space for those who don't always feel like they belong. From people of color to members of the LGBTQ+ community to those just considered *weird*, the X-books have been the entry point for many comic fans. And as one of the founding members of the X-Men, Jean Grey, along with her many aliases (Marvel Girl, the Phoenix, Redd, Ms. Psyche), has been an icon since the start.

At the age of ten Jean came into her mutant telepathic powers after experiencing the emotions of a dying friend. When Professor Xavier discovered the immense power that she possessed, he encouraged Jean to join his school in upstate New York, Xavier's School for Gifted Youngsters, and the recently formed super hero team, the X-Men. On her first mission, alongside the team's other founding members— Angel, Cyclops, Beast, and Iceman—she took on Magneto, a villainous mutant with magnetic powers.

The X-Men were successful in defeating their first enemy, proving they belonged in the ranks of Earth's defenders.

Back at school, Jean grew up with her fellow heroes and her teacher, Xavier, learning how to use her telepathic and telekinetic powers to support the X-Men's mission. But life is more than super hero battles, and as many teenagers do, Jean and Scott Summers, aka Cyclops, fell in love and later married.

Soon, though, her life and relationships would be put into jeopardy, when after a misadventure in space, Jean was possessed by the all-powerful Phoenix Force—an immortal and indestructible manifestation of the prime universal force of life. This alien entity gifted her with immense power, but over time corrupted her mind, eventually causing her to take her own life.

Of course, this is comics, so this would not be the end of the story for Jean Grey. She has returned time and time again, sometimes as the Phoenix, sometimes as the past or future version of herself, though always standing side by side with her fellow X-Men with the mind to use her powers to help those who are in need.

MEET THE COSPLAYER:

★ ★ INDRA ROJAS, @INDRA_ROJAS! ★ ★

ANY KID GROWING UP IN THE 1990S AND 2000S remembers this as the era of Saturday morning cartoons. For many soon-to-be Marvel fans, *X-Men: The Animated Series* on Fox Kids was their introduction to super heroes and the comic universe. But the X-Men were more than just super-powered, they were a group of teenagers learning how to be different in a society that didn't understand them. For Indra Rojas, I'm sure that feeling of being *different* rings true, after moving to the United States from Venezuela at the age of twelve.

It was through a different fandom that she was first introduced to cosplay, all the way back in 2004. "I was searching for a desktop wallpaper of a game I had just finished. I saw a photo of the main character and a singer with a tag 'the singer looks like he's cosplaying the main character.' I didn't understand the term, so when I looked it up, I found photos of cosplayers and was immediately intrigued!"

Although she had helped sew small craft projects for her mother's interior design business, she had minimal knowledge of what went into building a costume.

"There weren't very many tutorials or information back then, but I entered a lot of cosplay competitions, where I met cosplayers who shared their tips on how they would make certain things." Over the years, she pushed herself to learn new skills and try different materials. Now with more than twenty years of experience, cosplay has become a major part of her life, from her career to meeting her husband.

And as she grew from a comics-obsessed teen to an adult, Marvel has always been a passion for Indra. From her first Marvel cosplay, an Elektra costume, to the multitude of Marvel ladies, she never needs an excuse to make a new costume. "In high school, I naturally kept a Marvel calendar behind my door. When the Elektra month popped up, it was instant inspiration, and I knew I had to cosplay her! Since then, I've cosplayed many Marvel characters, with Lady Loki, Spider-Gwen, Black Cat, Jean Grey, Psylocke, and Magik being some of my favorites!"

Indra often is drawn to cosplay characters that inspire her. "I love how resilient, powerful, yet vulnerable and kind Jean is." So, with multiple versions of Jean Grey in her cosplay catalog, she jumped at the chance to tackle a new version: the Dark Phoenix. From the iconic Marvel Girl design to the original Phoenix suit, there is not one bad option to cosplay, so join Indra as she embarks on making her next Jean Grey costume.

Blending fabric and foam, Indra strikes a pose in her Magik cosplay.

"Jean's Phoenix transformation in the nineties cartoon is pretty much engraved into my brain—it was one of the coolest things I ever saw as a kid!"

—Indra Rojas

★ ★ JEAN GREY, AKA THE DARK PHOENIX ★ ★

COSPLAY BUILD NOTES

IN THIS NEXT BUILD, WE'LL BE CRAFTING FOUR ELE-ments of Jean Grey's Dark Phoenix costume, including a super suit, gloves, boot covers, and sash, plus styling her wig. You will use several techniques for this build that we used in Chapters 4 and 5, like patterning, sewing, and appliqué, as well as exploring two new techniques: crafting with foam and wig styling.

With the availability and wide selection of store-bought patterns, we'll use this to our advantage with this build and use two different ones for the suit and accessories. If the listed patterns are unavailable, then look to see what other options are available online or in store. It's also a good idea before sitting down to start your build to read through the pattern's instructions—and give your pattern pieces a pass with an iron to smooth out any folds or wrinkles.

This is our first build using EVA foam, a skill many cosplayers regularly use in their arsenal, for the phoenix emblem on the sash. As it's a smaller item, you can find smaller sheets of foam at your local craft store, or use a piece of thicker cardboard.

With wig styling, take care to check what level of heat your wig can be styled with. And for all cosplayers, you'll find what hair products work best for your styling, as we'll be using a spritz and not an aerosol for this styling. Also, depending on your hair, you may want to purchase a wig cap and bobby pins to secure the wig to your head.

MATERIAL LIST

SUIT, GLOVES, BOOT COVERS, AND SASH

- Patterns
  - *McCall's M7269 or similar pattern (bodysuit)*
  - *McCall's M7397 or similar pattern (gloves and boot covers)*
- 2 to 3 yards of black spandex
- 2 to 3 yards of red metallic spandex
- Black and red thread
- 22- to 24-inch black zipper
- Hook and eye (optional)

PHOENIX EMBLEM AND SASH PIN

- 2mm EVA foam
- HeatnBond Ultra Hold, or similar iron-on adhesive
- Alligator clip, pin back, or safety pin

PURCHASED ACCESSORIES

- Long auburn-colored wig with bangs
- Close-toe shoes, flats or heels

WIG CRAFTING ITEMS

- Foam or canvas head
- Brush
- Rattail comb
- Hair clips or duckbill hair clips
- Ultra-hold hair spray

ADDITIONAL SEWING AND CRAFT ITEMS

- Chalk or fabric marker
- Hair dryer
- Hot glue and glue sticks
- Iron, ironing board, and pressing cloth
- Pattern paper
- Pins
- Ruler
- Scissors
- Sewing machine

STEP-BY-STEP GUIDE

BUILDING THE SUPER SUIT PATTERN

1. Start by laying out your patterns and then cut. For this build, we are using:
   - **SUIT:** Pattern A, include front, back, sleeve, and collar.
   - **GLOVES:** Pattern J.
   - **BOOT COVERS:** Either Pattern B or Pattern C.
2. Before transferring to your fabric, adjust the patterns for any needed modifications. If you'd like to add in the pointed thigh seam of the boot cover, start on the left side of the pattern and measure 4½ inches down from the top of the pattern, and then draw a diagonal line from the upper right-hand corner to the measured mark.

   TIP: If this is your first time sewing a bodysuit, you can first cut and sew a mockup to better fit to your body. As an added bonus, you'll be able to refer to the mockup in the future.

3. Lay each pattern down on the corresponding fabric, right side down, and mark out the following:

BLACK STRETCH FABRIC:

- 1 front
- 2 back
- 2 sleeves

RED METALLIC STRETCH FABRIC:

- 4 gloves
- 4 boot covers

Transfer any lines and notches onto the fabric, label, then cut out all your pieces.

SEWING THE SUPER SUIT

1. Following the Pattern A instructions, with right sides together, pin the front piece to the left back piece at the side seams, then sew together. Repeat with the right back piece.

TIP: When using stretch fabric, aim to use a zigzag stitch; if you have one, a serger is a great way to stitch a spandex bodysuit together.

2. Next, sew the shoulders together by pinning the top of the front and back pieces, then sewing. Follow for both left and right sides.

3. Take the left and right back pieces, right sides facing, pin, and sew the back seam, starting from the inside leg seam to the designated notch at the end of the zipper.

4. To sew the legs, start with the right sides facing, pin the inside seams together, from the left ankle to the center crotch seams and then back down to the bottom of the right leg. Then stitch together.

TIP: When sewing high-stress areas like the crotch of the pants, you may want to pass over the area a second, or even third, time with your machine to ensure your seam is secure and prevent any costume malfunctions.

5. Before adding the sleeves, turn the suit right side out and check the fit. Mark and then make any necessary adjustments.

6. Start with the left sleeve and fold with right sides facing so it becomes a tube shape. Pin and stitch

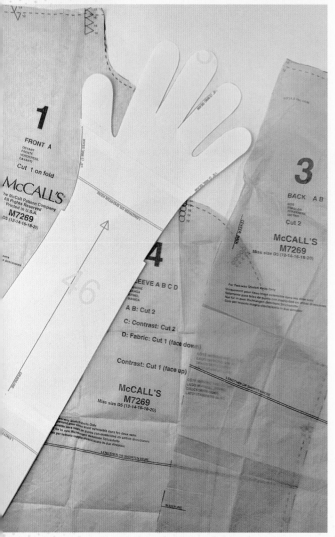

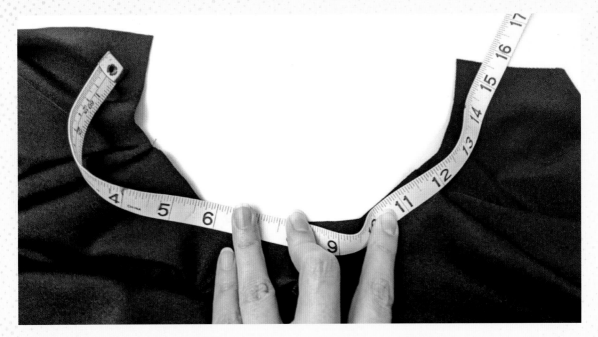

down the sleeve seam. Repeat with the right sleeve.

7. Turn both sleeves right side out. With right sides facing, pin each sleeve to the corresponding armhole, matching notches at the shoulder and underarm, then stitch together.

ADDING THE DETAILS

Now, we'll add the collar. Depending on your pattern, the bodysuits come with a piece for the collar. If not, you can create your own.

1. First, create the collar by measuring your collar length, then add 2 inches. Next, measure and mark a width of 3 inches. Then cut.
2. Fold the fabric strip horizontally, matching wrong sides together, pin, and then stitch to the collar of the bodysuit.

TIP: You can add fusible interfacing to the back of the collar if you'd like it to have more structure.

Next is installing the zipper.

3. Starting with the left side of the zipper, pin it to the bodysuit, and then, using your zipper foot, sew it on. Repeat with the right side of the zipper. If you'd like, you can hand-sew on a hook and eye to the top of the back collar above the zipper.

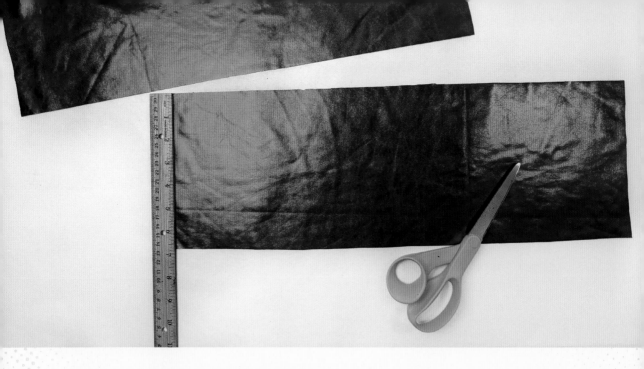

4. Turn the suit right side in, check the fit, and adjust any seams as needed. Then finish the wrist and ankle raw edges to your liking.

SEWING THE ACCESSORIES

First, we will build the gloves and then the boots.

1. Start by pinning the right sides together for both gloves, and then stitch each side seam.
2. Test the fit and then finish each lower-edge seam.
3. Follow the same process to sew the boot covers together. Next, pin and then sew the sole seams together for both covers.
4. Add a small piece of Velcro to the toe of your boot and its mate where it will touch the inside of the boot cover to prevent any movement.
5. Add a shoe grip inside the soles of the boot covers to prevent your feet from slipping as you walk.
6. Turn the boot covers right side out, test the fit with your shoes for the costume, and then finish the upper thigh seam edge.
    If your boot has a high heel, here is an extra step to help the cover fit perfectly:

7. Create a hole in the bottom of the cover to pull the heel of your shoe through; then paint the heel to match the fabric.
    Next, you'll build the sash.
8. First, measure the circumference of your waist or hips, depending on where the sash will sit, then measure from that point to your knees. Next, double your waist (or hip) to knee length and then add 10 inches.
9. For example, if your hip circumference is 38 inches and it is 18 inches from your hip to your knee, then your calculations would be: 38 + 18 + 18 + 10 = 84. The total length of the sash would be 84 inches.
10. Lay out your fabric, right side down, mark the desired length and 7 inches for the width. Then cut out the sash.

11. Fold the fabric in half widthwise, right sides together, pin, and then sew, creating a tube with both ends open.

12. Turn it right side out and finish the edges by tucking in the ends and top-stitching each edge.

TIP: You can make your sash wider, narrower, shorter, or longer depending on your desired look!

ADDING THE PHOENIX EMBLEMS

To finish the suit, we will create the phoenix emblems. You'll need two templates for the logos: a large version for the front of the suit, and a smaller one for the sash buckle, created either by hand or using a computer program.

1. Using red metallic fabric, lay down the templates, marking the design, and then carefully cut out the shapes.

2. Next, cut a piece of an iron-on adhesive, like HeatnBond, that is a little bit larger than the size of the phoenix emblems.

3. With a pressing cloth, iron the adhesive onto the back side of the fabric. Once cooled, trim any extra adhesive or fabric.

4. While wearing the suit, mark on the fabric where you'd like to position it, using either pins or chalk.

5. After removing the suit, peel the adhesive backing off the emblem and lay it back down onto your desired placement. Using a pressing cloth, iron the emblem on, securing each point and edge.

6. Depending on your final desired look, you can leave as is, or add a topstitch to the finalized emblem.

7. For the small phoenix design on the sash, repeat steps 1 through 3.

8. Then, using 2mm EVA foam, cut out a square—it should be a little larger than the template.

TIP: Keep your foam scraps, as you'll likely find a use for them in the future, such as for the phoenix design!

9. Peel the adhesive backing off your small fabric phoenix and place onto the foam. Cover with your pressing cloth, and then iron down.

10. If you see that your foam curls, keep the pressing cloth on the foam and wait for it to cool. You can also place a book or something heavy on it as it cools.

11. Cut closely around the edge of the design so that it looks like a solid inverted triangle.

12. Cut a little strip of foam to create a loop and hot glue it to the back. You can use this loop for your alligator clip, pin back, or safety pin to fasten it to the sash.

STYLING THE WIG

1. Pull the wig out of the bag, place onto the canvas or foam head, and securely pin it in place.

TIP: As an optional tool, you can use a wig styling stand, either standing or attached to a table to make it extra sturdy!

2. Brush the wig, removing any tangles or knots.

3. Divide the bangs in two—top and bottom—and pin back the top section by clipping it back to the top of the wig.

4. Back comb the bottom section of the bangs, going from tip to root. Repeat this process and separate the hair, so that the "knots" slide toward the cap.

5. Once it looks like a nest, apply hair spray generously, then use the hair dryer to lock the style in place. Point the dryer upward and fan the air back and forth until it is dry.

6. Brush out the "nest," so that you have a super textured poof. Use the clips to start shaping to create a heavy side bang. Spray, comb, and use the hair dryer as often as you need.

7. Once you have a good style base, undo all the clips and brush the top of the bangs onto the front. Spray and smooth with your hands, until you're left with a polished style.

THE FINAL LOOK

With the hair spray set, get ready for your final test fit! Pull on the suit, gloves, shoes, and boot covers. Tie the sash. And finally add the styled wig. Make any final adjustments, and then strike your fiercest pose for a photo or two. It's time to celebrate as you have successfully completed your Jean Grey, Dark Phoenix, cosplay!

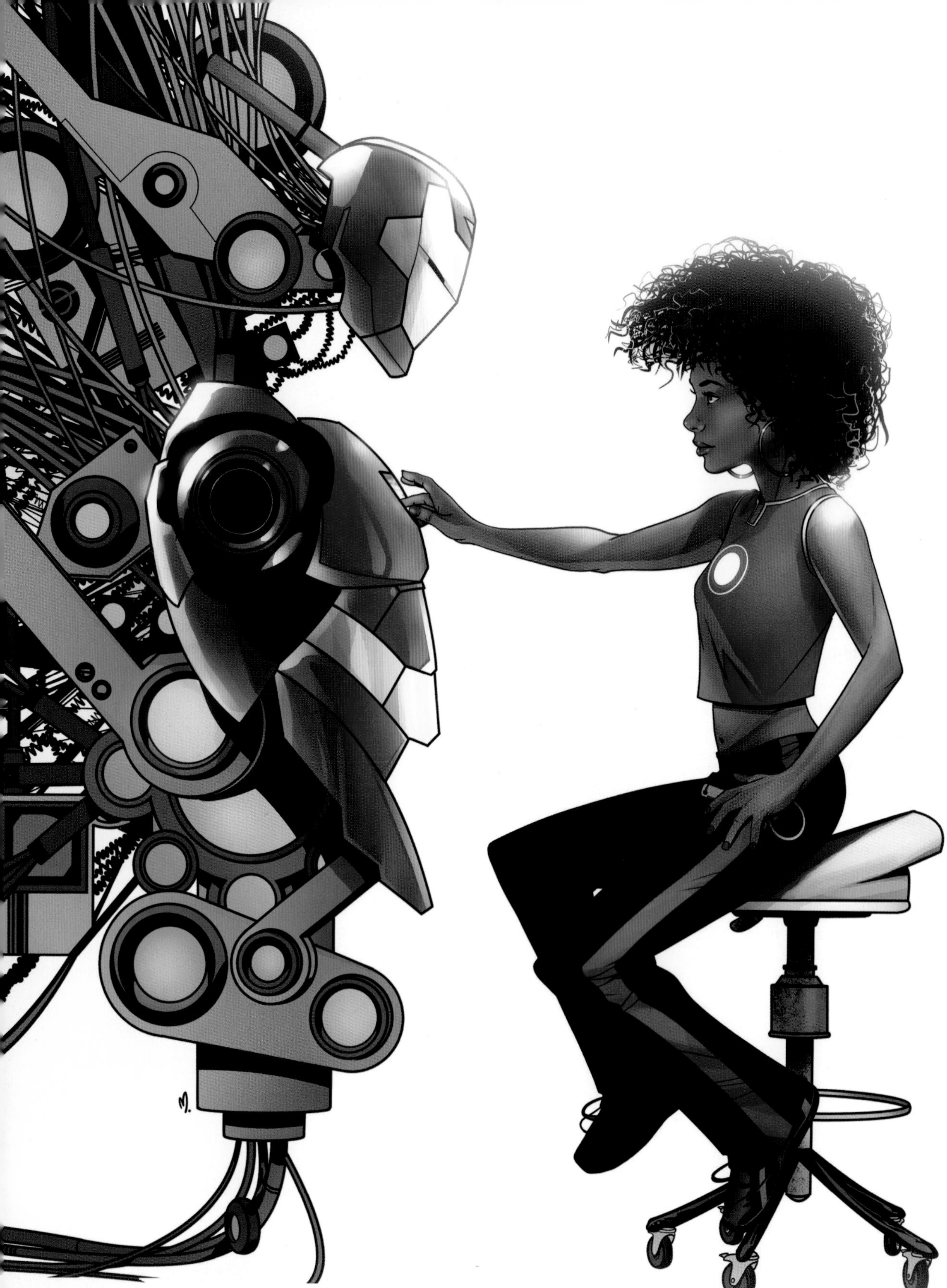

CHAPTER 7

One of Earth's Newest Heroes . . . Ironheart

★ ★ Who Is Riri Williams, aka Ironheart? ★ ★

"I was tired of being afraid. I wanted to fly."

THERE ARE A SELECT FEW SUPER GENIUSES IN THE Marvel Universe. You may know a few of them— Mr. Fantastic, Bruce Banner (when he's not the Hulk), Moon Girl, and of course Tony Stark. But there's now a new name to add to that list . . . Riri Williams, also known as Ironheart.

Far from the super hero headquarters of New York, Riri grew up in Chicago with her mother and stepfather after the death of her father, Demetrius, her namesake. From a very young age it was clear she was highly intelligent and more interested in inventing new and advanced machines than doing typical childhood things. But eventually, Riri would meet a best friend, Natalie, who encouraged her to be a *kid*, while also supporting her in her tinkering. Sadly, like many super hero stories, their friendship would end in tragedy. Just a few months after her thirteenth birthday, Natalie and Riri's stepfather were both killed in a random drive-by shooting while at a picnic. In one moment, Riri lost two of the most important people in her life.

Shutting out the pain, Riri threw herself into her work, graduating high school early, and then leaving home to attend Massachusetts Institute of Technology (MIT) at just fifteen years old. At MIT, Riri finally had access to a workshop, with the materials and tools

A-LERT. A-LERT. UNUSUAL POLICE ACTIVITY DETECTED IN PROXIMITY.

MAN, I NEED TO HURRY UP AND GET A REAL A.I.--THAT DISEMBODIED HAL VOICE IS WACK.

THANK YOU, COMPUTER. CAN YOU PLEASE CALL UP ANY RELEVANT NEWS FOOTAGE FROM THE LAST FEW MINUTES?

--GLOBAL SUMMIT IN UTTER CHAOS. RUMORS THAT THE NATIONAL GUARD--

OH BOY. WELL, BROKEN ARM CANNON, YOU'LL HAVE TO WAIT.

I NEED TO RUN DOWN THE STREET FOR A SECOND...

...AND THEN AFTER THIS, I REALLY DO NEED TO GET LUNCH.

to push her inventions even further. Inspired by Iron Man, she reverse engineers Tony Stark's designs in secret and builds herself her own suit of armor, using a few pieces stolen from the robotics lab. When campus security finally catches on, Riri puts on her armor and flies off, leaving MIT behind.

During her test flight across the country, Riri tries her hand at the super hero thing, catching two escaped inmates, but damaging her armor in the process. After returning to Chicago, she's surprised when she finds Tony Stark waiting for her. Impressed, Tony offers her an opportunity to join him in New York to better her engineering skills and learn how to use the suit.

With the support of Iron Man and later the super hero community, the still-teenage Riri decides to follow in the footsteps of her mentors and become a hero herself. And when Tony is injured during a super hero civil war, Riri steps up to take over the Iron Man mantle, becoming Ironheart. As she says in Issue #1 of *Ironheart*, "Those who move with courage make the path for those who live in fear." Marked by the tragedies in her past, Riri strives to use her intelligence, passion, and drive to protect her loved ones and to be the best hero she can be.

MEET THE COSPLAYER:

★ ★ KISA WATTON, @KIZUKI_COSPLAY! ★ ★

WE HEAD ACROSS THE POND TO THE UNITED KINGDOM to meet our next cosplayer, Kisa Watton. Cosplay is truly a worldwide phenomenon, with relatable experiences happening from continent to continent. For example, we each remember that first magical experience of seeing cosplayers out in the wild, and for Kisa, it was watching a cosplay competition with her mother at a local convention. There seems to be a consistent theme appearing, as each cosplayer grew up in a home filled with a passion for crafting. From her mother encouraging her to lean into her fandom, and having an art teacher as a father, there was no limit to Kisa's exploration as a child.

It was 2013 when she first dipped her toes into cosplay, starting out from an interest in anime and video games. Then for her first Marvel costume, she decided to challenge herself with a female version of the Falcon. "Actually, a friend's mother helped me sew the leggings, and then I spent hours gluing red feathers to make his wings." Now, more than ten years later, she can say she has an extensive Marvel cosplay catalog, tackling more than twenty-five costumes, including

Kisa finds a good backdrop and the perfect lighting in her Shuri cosplay.

"It's crazy to think about all the friends that I have made here in the UK and across the world. I get to travel and have all these amazing experiences just because of one small interaction complimenting another's costume, that lead to more and creates a beautiful friendship."

—Kisa Watton

Misty Knight, Iron Man, Storm, Ultron, Heimdall, and Makkari. Personally, I think her personal achievement is creating multiple versions of a character, especially having four Shuri cosplays and even four Miles Morales cosplays!

For many of these costumes, she was part of a group of old friends, or even new ones. "Some of my favorite moments at con are when you turn up in a costume by yourself, but then by the end of the day you have a full squad of friends who also happen to be cosplaying from the same show! Everyone gets to vibe together, and honestly this is how I've made the majority of my lifelong friends."

Building on her art-filled childhood, through the last decade she has continued to accumulate a wide variety of skills. "Most of my early knowledge came from blogs and old YouTube videos. And then experimenting with anything accessible in local art stores. Thus, a lot of my earlier costumes were created using very basic methods." And now with a degree in 3D design, along with the many years of soaking up fellow cosplayers' knowledge, she looks to tackle more and more challenging projects.

Which leads us to Kisa creating an armored super suit. As a fellow admirer of science and math, plus a Tony Stark fan, cosplaying Riri Williams was an easy decision for her. "Seeing an intelligent, fun, young black woman wearing an Iron Man suit is a dream for me." As Kisa had done a version of Riri before, she was excited to return to the character.

So, no matter where in the world you are, get ready to join Kisa as she breaks down the steps to create the newest armored hero, Ironheart.

★ ★ RIRI WILLIAMS, AKA IRONHEART ★ ★

COSPLAY BUILD NOTES

FOR THIS BUILD, WE'LL BE EXPLORING THE MAGICAL world of foam and 3D printing by crafting two elements of Riri's armor—the arc reactor and gauntlet—along with sewing her red crop top. Additionally, we purchased a pair of pants, but you can craft your own if you'd like.

For any 3D elements, it's important to finalize the design and determine which techniques and materials will work best before you get started. For this cosplay, we'll be using different techniques for each. For the gauntlet, we'll be making it out of foam, as it's more flexible, and then we'll be 3D printing the arc reactor. (You can learn more about 3D printing on page 98.) Remember, as you transform a 2D comic book design into 3D, there may be some adjusting required, for both esthetics and logistics.

When working with foam, you'll want to be sure you are using a sharp craft knife and applying even pressure and consistent speed to ensure a smooth line as you cut out each piece of foam. The cut of your foam will depend a lot on the angle you hold your knife, which should be a perfect straight line coming from a 90-degree hold. If you want a bevel, using a ruler, angle the blade toward the ruler while cutting.

For glue, there are several options you can use depending on your build material, but we'll be using contact cement, mainly because it is more flexible and forgiving. Not all foam has to be primed and sealed, but it will help it retain its shape and prevent the paint from chipping. Like glue, there are many different products out there for priming foam, but we'll be using wood glue—it's cheap, accessible, and it gives a nice glossy finish.

For the arc reactor, the cosplayer used their personal 3D printer, but you can also look into maker spaces or your local universities to see if they have a printer available for use, or you can commission a print from a fellow cosplayer with a printer. The printer used for this build is one of the more popular types of

3D printers for the printed piece—a large-volume LCD resin printer that uses a screen to selectively project UV light into a tank of UV resin to print the object. Like the other 3D-printed pieces in this book, you can create your own print files or look online for fully designed files. We'll be using a model by Sionnach Studios for this arc reactor.

MATERIAL LIST

GAUNTLET
- Plastic wrap
- Duct tape
- 1 sheet of 4mm EVA foam
- 1 sheet of 2mm EVA foam
- Contact cement
- PVA wood glue
- Black spray paint
- Red and gold acrylic flexible paint
- Sealant
- ½ yard of black jersey or spandex

ARC REACTOR
- 3D model
- Black spray paint
- Silver Rub 'n Buff
- 4mm white Plastazote foam
- Blue acrylic paint
- White metallic spray paint
- Magnetic purse snaps
- Contact cement

CROP TOP
- 1 yard of red scuba or jersey fabric; it should have some structure or weight
- Red thread

PURCHASED ITEMS
- Black pants

ADDITIONAL SEWING AND CRAFTING ITEMS
- 3D printer with any added tools
- Chalk
- Colored markers
- Craft knife or blade
- Paintbrushes
- Pattern paper
- Pins
- Ruler
- Scissors
- Scotch tape
- Sewing machine

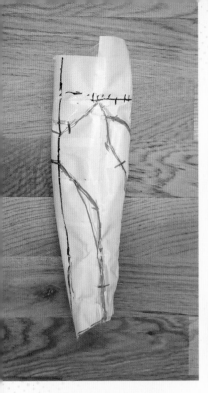 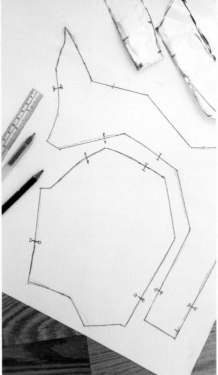 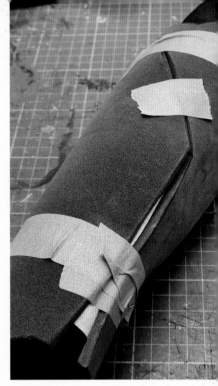

THE GAUNTLET PATTERN

To ensure the gauntlet will fit your arm, you'll first want to create a mold of your forearm, using plastic wrap and then duct tape.

1. Start by creating a mold of your forearm by first wrapping your arm, from the wrist to up past your elbow, with plastic wrap, then with duct tape.

2. Draw a vertical line down the inside of your arm, then mark the top and bottom by drawing horizontal lines at your wrist and elbow.

3. Sketch out the design of the center and the outer part of the bracer using different colored markers, making sure to label each piece.

4. Carefully cut off the duct tape mold of your arm with a pair of scissors.

5. Cut out each shape from your mold, then transfer it to pattern paper, copying any notes to create a template.

TIP: Transferring patterns to pattern paper will ensure the longevity of the pattern in case you want to use it again in the future. It is also easier to trace onto foam or fabric.

6. For the armored "ring" pieces for your fingers, draft a small rectangle, rounding out the corners.

7. When finished, you should have the following pattern pieces:
   - Center forearm bracer
   - Outer forearm bracer
   - Hand plate
   - Thumb plate
   - Finger ring

8. Next, trace each shape onto the foam, along with any notches and notes.

USING THE 4MM FOAM:

- 1 center forearm bracer
- 1 outer forearm bracer
- 1 hand plate
- 1 thumb plate

USING THE 2MM FOAM:

- 13 finger rings
1. With a sharp craft knife or blade, begin to cut out each shape.
2. To double-check the gauntlet fit, assemble all the pieces, using Scotch tape, to ensure they all fit together and that you'll still be able to move your hand and wrist.

ASSEMBLING THE GAUNTLET

We'll start by building the bracer.

1. Begin prepping for assembly by applying contact cement to both sides of the seams of the center and outer bracer pieces. Wait about five minutes until the glue stops being tacky, then carefully press the seams together, making sure that the marks line up.

TIP: For any glue or paint, take note of the safety instructions for each product, and wear a respirator and gloves when needed.

2. Prime the bracer using a coat of the wood glue.
3. Once the prime coat is dry, seal the foam using a spray primer, and then apply a coat of black paint.
4. Next, paint the gauntlet using flexible acrylic paints, using various shades of red to create detail.
5. After the paint has dried, add a clear coat of sealant.
   Next, we'll be creating a glove out of black jersey fabric for the base of our gauntlet.
6. Place your hand down on a sheet of pattern paper and then trace the shape of your hand, wrist, and forearm, spreading your fingers to leave a ½-inch gap between each.
7. Cut out the pattern.

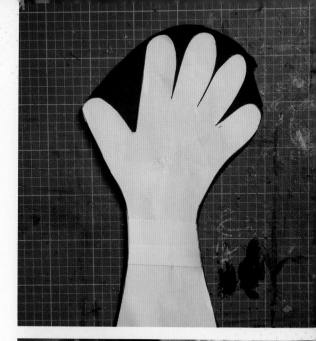

8. Fold your jersey fabric in half, then transfer the pattern to the fabric, then cut.
9. Pin along the outline and then stitch.
10. Test the fit, then cut and trim the excess fabric around the seam.
11. Turn the glove right side out, test the fit once more, and then finish the edge.

    With the foam bracer and black glove completed, now we will combine them using contact cement.
12. Apply contact cement to the inside of the bracer and wait about five minutes until the glue stops being tacky. Then, while wearing the glove, carefully slide the glove into the bracer and press to secure the bracer to the glove.
13. Next, glue each of the rings for the fingers, starting with the tips and moving toward the hand, so they'll lay smoothly on top of one another.
14. Finish the assembly by gluing on the hand and thumb plates.

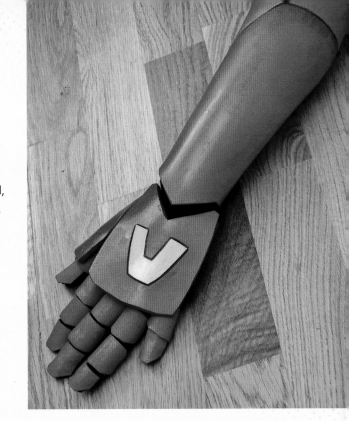

BUILDING THE ARC REACTOR

1. Start by following the printing directions for your specific 3D printer, then, using the model, begin printing the top piece of the arc reactor.
2. Once the print has finished, remove the piece and sand down any rough edges. If needed, you can use a primer to further smooth out the piece.
3. Add a layer of black spray paint.
4. Paint on a layer of silver Rub 'n Buff.
5. Measure and cut out a piece of white Plastazote or EVA foam for the back of the reactor.
6. Add a layer of blue acrylic paint and then add a light layer of white metallic spray paint on the Plastazote.
7. After the paint has dried on both pieces, assemble by gluing the 3D-printed piece to the top of the Plastazote using contact adhesive.

BUILDING THE CROP TOP

As we did when crafting the Ms. Marvel tunic in Chapter 4, we'll use an existing shirt to create the pattern for the crop top.

1. Fold your shirt in half lengthwise and lay it on your pattern paper, then trace the shape.
2. Make any adjustments and add a ½-inch seam allowance and label.
3. Cut out the pattern.

TIP: If you have the time and extra scrap fabric, test the fit for the top before cutting into your fashion fabric.

4. Fold your scuba fabric in half, then transfer the pattern to the fabric, then cut.
5. Starting with the side seams, match right sides together, then pin and sew. Repeat with the shoulders.
6. Test the fit and then finish the raw edges of the neck, arms, and bottom to your liking.

ATTACHING THE ARC REACTOR

For easy transport and to fix when needed, we'll attach the reactor using two magnetic purse snaps.

1. While wearing the crop top, mark with chalk or pins where you want the arc reactor to sit and the location of the two magnetic snaps.
2. Mark where the corresponding snaps will go on the back of the arc reactor.
3. Remove the top and cut two small holes for each of the snaps.
4. With a needle and thread, hand-sew one side of each of the snaps onto the shirt.
5. Then, using contact cement, glue the other side of the snap to the back of the arc reactor. Remember to wait until the glue has dried before testing out the snaps, or they may detach from the arc reactor.

THE FINAL LOOK

With your three elements finished, add your pants and give them a whirl around your room, snapping a few photos. Be proud, because you've tackled two new skills: foam work and 3D printing. A round of congratulations is in order for completing your Ironheart cosplay!

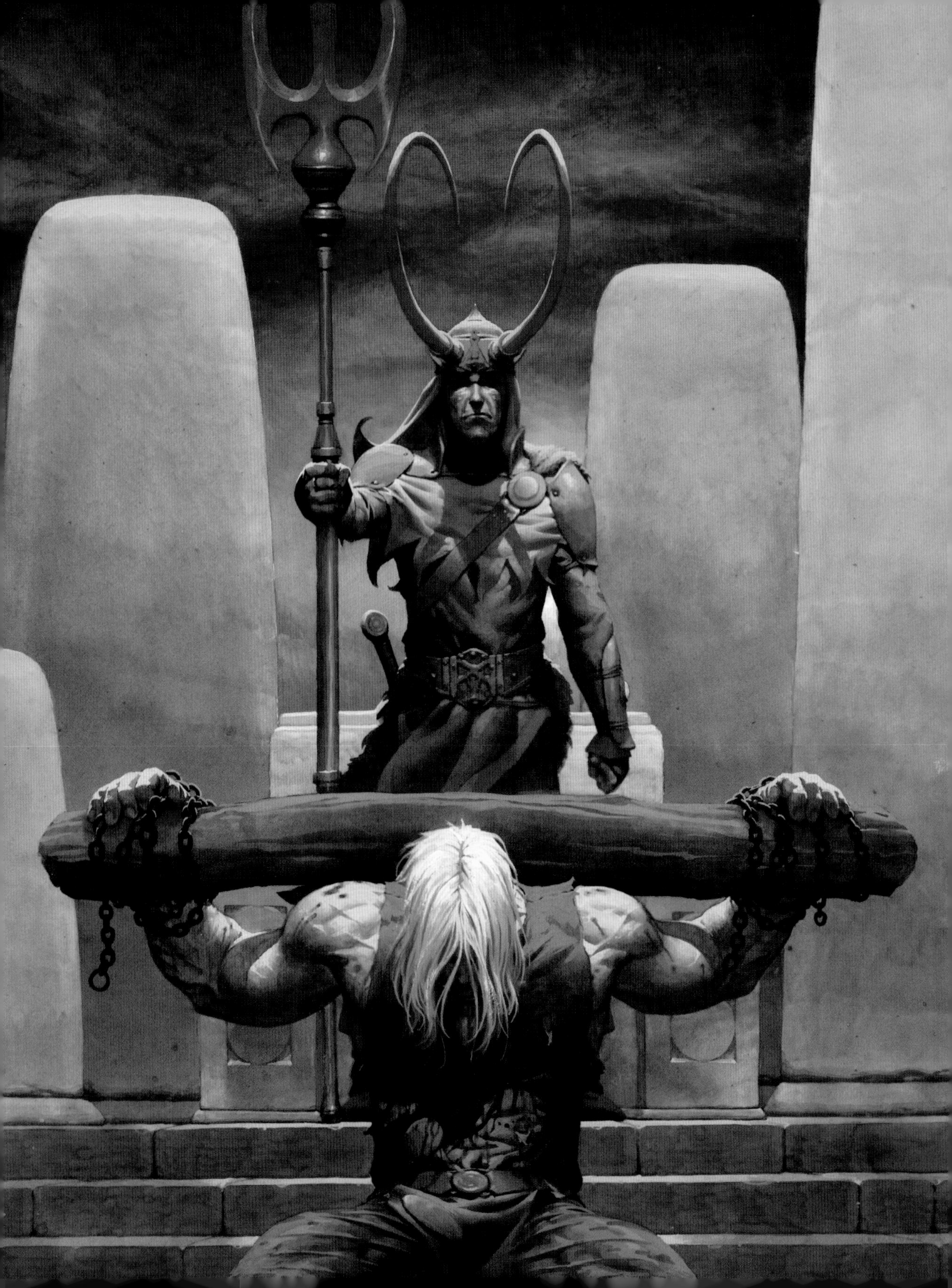

CHAPTER 8

The Magical and Mischievous Loki

★ ★ A Little Bit of Magic—Meet Loki ★ ★

"Mischief is a small thing, a toy I've well used and discarded.
This isn't mischief. This is mayhem. Just watch."

IN BETWEEN THE MANY SUPER HEROES AND SUPER villains, there stand those who hover over their own version of right and wrong: the anti-hero. And at the front, leading the pack, is the magical and scheming Loki, God of Mischief. You may know his more famous and iconic hammer-wielding brother, Thor of Asgard, but Loki has made himself known to Earth and their mightiest heroes through a mix of sorcery, deception, and guile.

Going back more than a thousand years ago, Loki was rescued by King Odin from his home realm of Jotunheim, after being abandoned by the Frost Giant King Laufey. After slaying Laufey, Odin returned to Asgard with Loki, and raised him alongside his son, Thor. But it was constantly witnessing the loving relationship between his brother and father that sparked jealousy and the need for retaliation. Loki would diverge from the path initially destined for him alongside his brother, channeling his anguish into plotting a way to beat Thor and become the next ruler of Asgard.

As the years passed, Loki used his aptitude for magic and sorcery, including shapeshifting, telepathy, hypnosis, and teleportation, to scheme and plot, first to thwart his brother and the people of Asgard, and then turning his attention to his next marks, far away on Midgard. In a plot to trick Thor into battling the Hulk, Loki was thwarted when Iron Man, Wasp,

Ant-Man, Hulk, and Thor joined powers to defeat him, inadvertently forming a new heroic group—the Avengers.

Though he may have been beaten down, Loki did not give up on his goal of claiming the throne. He would return time and time again with new schemes, wreaking havoc across the realms, and along the way crossing paths with many heroes and villains. However, once in a blue moon, you could even find him on the side of good. Maybe it was the repeated moments of failure, or even a growth in maturity,

but in those times of need, Loki lent a hand to help the heroes. But, of course, he could never lose his natural trickery and inevitably reverted to his more wicked ways.

But it's this nonlinear path that has endeared him to new fans of comics, helped by his role in the films and as a LGBTQ+ super-powered individual. He may have the power to play with fellow gods, but really, he's just like the rest of us, trying to make his parents proud. Although with a little bit of magical mischief.

★ ★ MARC SCHWERIN, @ELEGANTFEATHERDUSTER! ★ ★

IN THE 2000S, IT SEEMED LIKE THERE WAS A GENERAL awareness of Marvel and super hero comics in the cosplay community, but that all changed with the release of *Iron Man* in 2008, and then the ensuing Marvel Studios films, all leading to *The Avengers*. Suddenly, many cosplayers like Marc Schwerin had a new way to interact with Marvel's heroes, saying, "Oh, this is a whole universe. And it all connects."

When Marc drafted his first Marvel costume, a *Young Avengers* Loki, he had been creating his own costumes for some time. He had gotten started in 2005 as a teenager, borrowing his mother's sewing machine (she made quilts) and descending into the basement, then reappearing after lots of hard work with his first costume. Around this time, he started attending local anime conventions, but it wasn't until after moving to the East Coast for college that he discovered and started to engage with the cosplay community.

"By chance, I went to Boston Comic Con with some college friends in my Loki cosplay, and somebody came up to me and said, 'Oh, dope costume, are you going to the Marvel shoot later?' So, I did." From there, he met his first cosplay friends and found the support and encouragement to do so many, many more Marvel costumes. With more than a dozen different Tony Stark and Iron Man cosplays—plus Doctor Strange, Steve Rogers, Captain Marvel, Peter Parker, Magneto, just to name a few—Marc has become a familiar face within the Marvel cosplay scene.

He was also one of the early adopters of 3D printing for accessories and has gone on to build an extensive list of skills working with materials ranging from soft to hard. One of my earliest memories of Marc was seeing him at a Marvel Costume Contest at New York Comic Con; he had printed a bunch of 3D elements for his Avengers group. Even now, he is the go-to person

Witness the magic of a cape flip for the camera as Marc flies high in his Wiccan cosplay.

"My first real stab at a Marvel costume was actually the Jamie McKelvie *Young Avengers* Loki design back when that and *Agent of Asgard* were first coming out—so this is both a remake and a costume that's close to my heart."

—Marc Schwerin

for crafting props, plus helping to organize crews for costumes and photo shoots.

"I'm incredibly grateful for the often collaborative nature of cosplay. I've done things like hike mountains, stand outside in subzero weather, cover myself in fake blood, and saw mannequins in half (while my neighbors watched) just to make wild, interesting, hilarious, beautiful things with other creatives, many of whom became my friends. There is nothing quite like the joy of creating art with the people who matter most to you."

That level of dependability and expertise is priceless in this community, which was why it was an easy choice to invite him to join this book, especially to revisit one of his original Marvel costumes, Loki. "Loki is such an incredibly fun character—sometimes good, sometimes bad, usually something in between," says Marc. "And when it comes to *Young Avengers* Loki, what's not to love about the leather, black nail polish, and eyeliner that serve for the teenage goth in our hearts?"

And although there is no actual magic in this book, Marc is here to take you on a journey to learn the wizardry of 3D printing and offer some advice for crafting the trickster himself, Jamie McKelvie's *Young Avengers* Loki.

★ ★ LOKI ★ ★

COSPLAY BUILD NOTES

IN THIS PROJECT, YOU'LL BE BUILDING ON ALL YOUR previous skills as you craft Loki's coat and accessories, his helm and greaves, as well as a knife and sword. This project combines a variety of techniques including sewing, 3D printing, and painting. As this costume is heavy on the time-consuming prop and accessory making, we'll start with the 3D elements, and then work on the sewing pieces while they print.

You can often find print-ready 3D models online, but we'll be modeling and printing the 3D pieces, including the helm, greaves, sword, dagger, and collar decoration. While we want the pieces to be both accurate and beautiful, it is important to consider practical aspects: the helm has to be lightweight and comfortable, but placing delicate objects on boots or shoes is asking for trouble, so the greaves can't be too delicate. The sword is far too large to print as one piece and has to be broken down into manageable pieces. Almost all the objects needed to accommodate decoration, like leather, straps, and buckles, would be added later.

When deciding between spray paint versus acrylic, please keep ventilation in mind. You can find small, at-home spray booths available online, or spray outside with a safe setup. If you're limited by your options for healthy ventilation, a great alternate option for 3D prints is to use acrylic paints.

To cut down on some of the crafting time, we chose to purchase garments and modify them to match the design. A simple green tunic found online worked for the shirt, while we thrifted a pair of leather pants. For the gloves, we purchased a pair of simple black gloves, removed the fingers, and accessorized them with scrap pieces of leather and buckles. Then for the coat,

we used a faux-military coat as a base before adding in the desired modifications.

For finishing elements, like belts and buckles, you can purchase prefabricated options, though it's often more budget-friendly to use scrap leather and purchased hardware, plus it allows for better color consistency across all elements of the costume.

Finally, for the scalemail, we assembled the front, back, and leg pieces with aluminum scales and rings using traditional techniques and then painted each piece with spray paint. As this is a more advanced skill, alternatively you can purchase pre-assembled pieces or mimic the look using fabric or foam. For a detailed description of creating scalemail the traditional way, head online and check out tutorials there.

3D PRINTER BASICS

We used two of the more popular types of 3D printers for the printed pieces. The first is a fused deposition modeling, or FDM, printer, which is a type of extrusion printer that uses a corn-derived thermoplastic called PLA and prints layer by layer to form the object. The second is an LCD resin printer (also known as MSLA or masked stereolithography) that uses a screen to selectively project UV light into a tank of UV resin to print the object.

Because these two types of printers (and the prints they produce) have different strengths and weaknesses when it comes to things like speed, build volume, detail, and cost per part, it's best to pick which to use based on the needs for the piece. A finished prop can use both FDM parts for larger, lighter, simpler shapes and resin pieces for small areas with a lot of detail.

It's a good idea to use a high-strength, two-part adhesive designed for plastics both to glue the prints together and to fill any large gaps or holes to prepare the surface for painting. But some cosplayers also use products like super glue, automotive gap filler, wood putty, resin, or other materials to smooth their print surfaces. Just remember to always look at the safety information for products like these and wear protection as needed, since many of them can be hazardous.

MATERIAL LIST

3D-PRINTED PIECES
- 3D modeling software or print-ready files
- 3D printer and PLA plastic filament
- Epoxy or other 3D print-friendly glue
- Range of sandpaper from 60 to 320 grit
- Sandable spray filler-primer
- Spray or acrylic paint in gloss black, gloss clear, metallic gold, and metallic silver
- Adhesive vinyl or sticker paper (optional)

DETAILS AND ACCESSORIES
- Leather or fabric
  - 1½ yards of brown faux suede
  - 1 yard of gold fabric cut into 1½- to 2-inch-wide strips
- ¼ to ½ hide of green leather or 1 to 2 yards faux green leather
- ¼ to ½ hide of brown leather or ½ yard faux brown leather
- ½ yard white faux fur or a ready-made fur collar
- Notions
  - 4 brown leather closures with small gold buckles
  - 3 medium leather closures with gold buckles
  - 1 large leather closure with a gold buckle
  - ½ yard of 1-inch-wide elastic

PURCHASED GARMENTS AND ACCESSORIES

- Short black wig
- Long-sleeved green shirt
- Long green coat
- Black pants
- Black gloves
- Calf-height black boots
- 2 brown belts with gold buckles

ADDITIONAL SEWING AND CRAFTING ITEMS

- Chalk or marker
- Fabric glue
- Leatherworking supplies
- Pattern paper
- Painter's tape
- Pins
- Ruler
- Scissors
- Sewing machine
- Velcro or snaps

STEP-BY-STEP GUIDE

3D MODELING, PREPARING, AND PRINTING

Starting at a computer, draft or source digital versions of the armor, props, and accessories using 3D modeling software. You'll be printing the following pieces:

HELM

- 1 left side
- 1 right side
- 1 center decoration

COLLAR DECORATION, 2 GREAVES, AND A DAGGER

- 1 blade
- 1 hilt
- 1 pommel

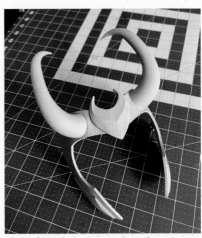

SWORD

- 1 sword blade point
- 1 middle of blade
- 1 base of blade
- 1 cross-guard
- 1 hilt
- 1 pommel

1. Export each 3D model as a watertight .stl file and load it into your 3D printer's software to slice, support, and prepare the model for print.
2. Once the prints have finished, glue together the pieces of the helm and sword. You'll assemble the dagger after painting.
3. Sand down any rough edges on all the 3D prints. If needed, you can use a primer to fill in any unwanted gaps.

TIP: 3D prints can also be modified after they're printed by cutting, denting, drilling, or heat-forming them.

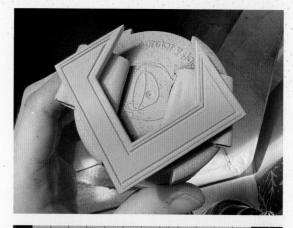

PRIMING, SANDING, AND PAINTING

1. Begin by spraying on several coats of a sandable filler-primer to smooth out the textured surface of the fully assembled helm and sword, as well as the collar decoration, two greaves, and the pieces of the dagger.
2. Next, sand any surface you're planning to paint until it is smooth.
   - Using a wet cloth, remove any sanding residue before painting.
   - Prep each piece for painting by starting with a layer of black spray paint.

   Then for each element, follow the steps below for painting:

TIP: For sandpaper, start with a dry sand at around 60 grit, and progress up to an ultra-fine wet sand like 320 grit to smooth out the surface of a print.

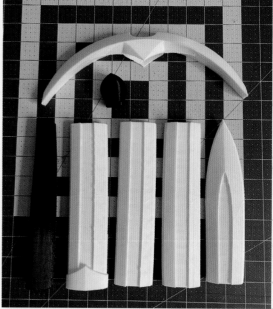

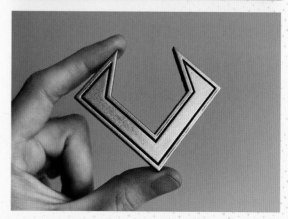

HELM, COLLAR DECORATION, GREAVES, AND DAGGER POMMEL:

Start with a layer of metallic gold spray paint, then add a layer of high-gloss clear spray paint. Finish with one more layer of metallic gold spray paint.

DAGGER BLADE:

Start with a layer of metallic silver spray paint, then add a layer of high-gloss clear spray paint. Finish with one more layer of metallic silver spray paint.

SWORD:

1. Using painter's tape and paper towel, tape off the cross-guard, hilt, and pommel so only the blade is exposed.
2. Paint the blade silver following the same process as for the blade of the dagger.
3. Remove the painter's tape from the cross-guard and pommel leaving it on the hilt.
4. Tape off the bottom of the blade, about 10 inches down.
5. Paint the cross-guard and pommel gold following the process for the helm.
6. Remove the painter's tape from the hilt.
7. Add the gold Norse-inspired knotwork detail in the sword's fuller, either by hand-painting the design, or by creating a stencil using adhesive vinyl or sticker paper cut by hand or with a cutting machine. With the sticky stencil placed on the sword, tape off any exposed blade, then spray on a layer of metallic gold paint.

TIP: All paints behave and interact with each other differently; it's always worth testing your paints on scrap pieces before you paint your prop!

FINISHING THE 3D ELEMENTS

DAGGER

1. Assemble the dagger by gluing the two pieces of the hilt and pommel together with the blade.
2. For the hilt, measure and cut out a rectangular shape from the green leather.
3. After soaking the leather in water, wrap it around the hilt, and using a thick string or thread, hand-stitch the leather closed.
4. To create the sheath, lay the dagger down on the brown leather. Measure around blade, adding a 1-inch seam allowance to each side, then cut. Using this as a pattern, cut out the second side of the sheath. Then sew them together by hand or machine with right sides out, leaving the top open.

SWORD

1. Measure and cut out a long strip of green leather. Length and width will be determined by the size of your sword, but we used a 1-inch by 36-inch strip.
2. After soaking the leather in water, wrap it around the hilt, creating a layering look, before sealing the end with glue.

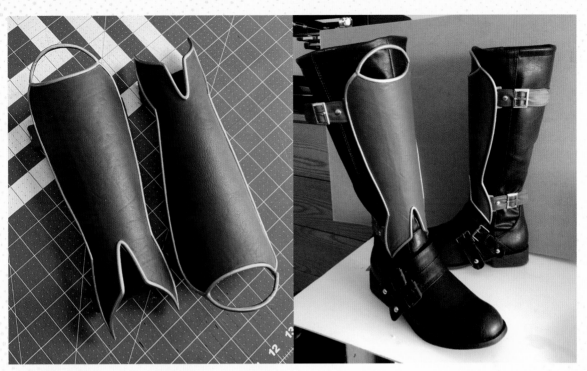

GREAVES

1. Measure and cut out two brown leather shapes for the greaves. Then glue down each leather shape, trimming any excess leather. Alternatively, you can also use brown paint to create the finished look.
2. Attach buckle closures to the back of the greaves using glue, or hand-stitch them.

SCALEMAIL

1. Assemble the scalemail for the front, back, and leg pieces with aluminum scales and rings. Then finish with a layer of green spray paint.

MODIFICATIONS FOR LOKI'S COAT

To match the design of Loki's coat, we'll be using crafted pieces to add detail to a pre-existing garment.

1. Start by removing any of the existing buttons or details, if there are any, that are not needed.

TIP: When using a thrifted or pre-worn item, it's always a good idea to give it a wash before beginning modifications.

2. For the lapels, cuffs, and back of the collar, first measure and create mock-up panels for each part, using either pattern paper or scrap fabric.

3. To add even more detail, you can use strips of the fabric to create a braided texture or, alternatively, use a solid piece of fabric.

4. Using the mock-ups as a pattern, transfer and cut out pieces of the brown faux suede.

5. Using the precut strips of gold fabric, fold the edges under and pin to the visible edges of each of the brown faux suede pieces, then stitch using your sewing machine.

6. Using the remaining precut gold fabric strips, follow the same process as above to add trim to the edges of the coat, including the front closure, sleeves, and bottom hem.

7. Using a strong fabric glue, attach each piece to the coat.

8. Finally, attach the white fur collar made from the white faux fur or use a ready-made one.

FINAL ACCESSORY DETAILS

1. To keep the belts at the waist from shifting, add Velcro or a snap to the cross points on the front and back.

2. Measure the circumference of your forehead and cut out the needed length of elastic. Glue each end of the elastic to the inside of the helm.

3. Attach the three pieces of scalemail to the pants and tunic, using leftover leather scraps to reinforce.

THE FINAL LOOK

Congratulations on learning even more new crafting skills! Pull on the shirt, pants, coat, gloves, boots, belts, and helm. Finally, after a quick brushing, top it all with the black wig. This may be your first time wearing every piece, so take a moment to see how it feels all together, and if you need to make any final adjustments to the look or feel of the costume. Finally, put on a coat of black nail polish, and you are ready to get into some trouble as Loki!

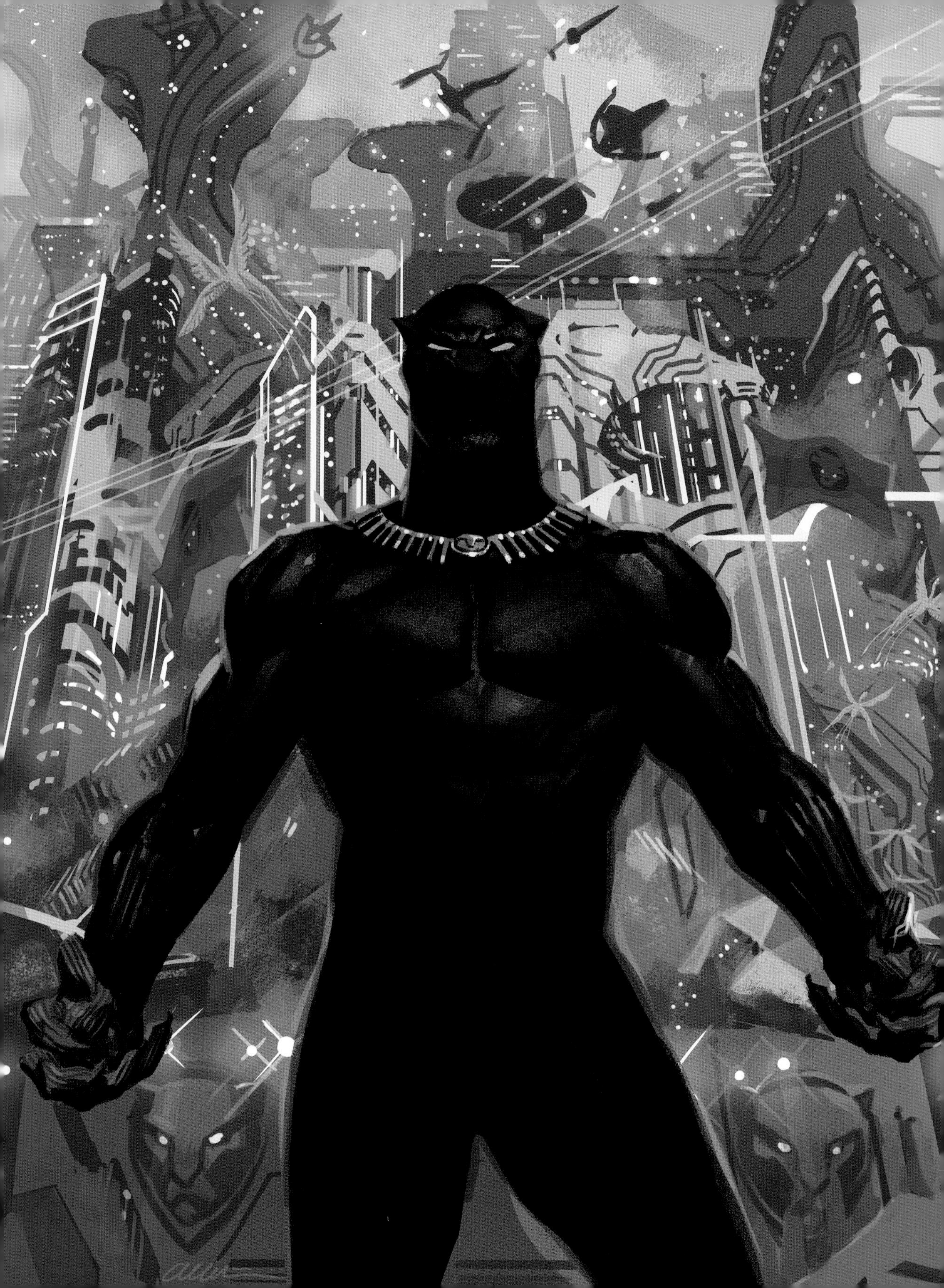

CHAPTER 9

A King and a Warrior— He Is the Black Panther

"Take your best shot. I will offer no resistance.
Then it will be my turn."

THE FIRST AFRICAN HERO IN THE PAGES OF MARVEL Comics, T'Challa is the current king of Wakanda, a highly advanced African nation, as well as the powerful warrior known as the Black Panther. Following in the footsteps of his forefathers, the Black Panther is granted extra abilities by the Panther God upon proving him or herself worthy in a combat tournament.

The son of King T'Chaka, the incredibly intelligent T'Challa came into his birthright after his father was killed by the villainous Ulysses Klaw. But before he took on the mantle of Black Panther, first, he traveled the world, learning about fellow super heroes, then returned to his homeland to challenge his uncle for the throne. With his uncle defeated, T'Challa took his rightful place in the community, and received the special heart-shaped herbs that would grant him enhanced strength and senses.

Before T'Challa's reign, Wakanda had remained hidden and secretive for generations because of the unique power contained within its borders. Their greatest natural resource, vibranium, a rare vibration-absorbing metal, allowed the nation to covertly advance its own technology, including creating the Black Panther suit. Though it has changed in design over the years, the suit has always featured vibranium enhancements that absorb impacts, from physical blows to gunshots, and pads in the feet and hands that allow for easier climbing.

Unlike his predecessors, T'Challa ventured out into the world, sharing the passion and technological superiority of his people. He also chose to join the Earth's mightiest heroes to become a hero around the world and beyond. At times he's been a part of the Avengers, Fantastic Four, and the secretive Illuminati while also ruling a nation and looking for love and a queen, for a time, in the X-Men's Storm.

In addition to his super-powered friends, T'Challa is served by his female bodyguards, the Dora Milaje. Chosen from each of the eighteen tribes of Wakanda, the "adored ones" are some of the most formidable fighters in the world. The Black Panther relies on these lethal women to come to his aid when needed, and they would sacrifice everything to protect Wakanda and its people.

Standing at his side is another fierce warrior, his younger sister, Shuri. A fantastic genius scientist, Shuri has used her skills to mastermind new weapons and innovations. At one point, taking the battle out into the world, she stepped up to temporarily become the Black Panther when her brother was wounded.

With his family and people behind him, T'Challa stands tall as the Black Panther: a righteous king, fearsome warrior, and one of Earth's mightiest heroes.

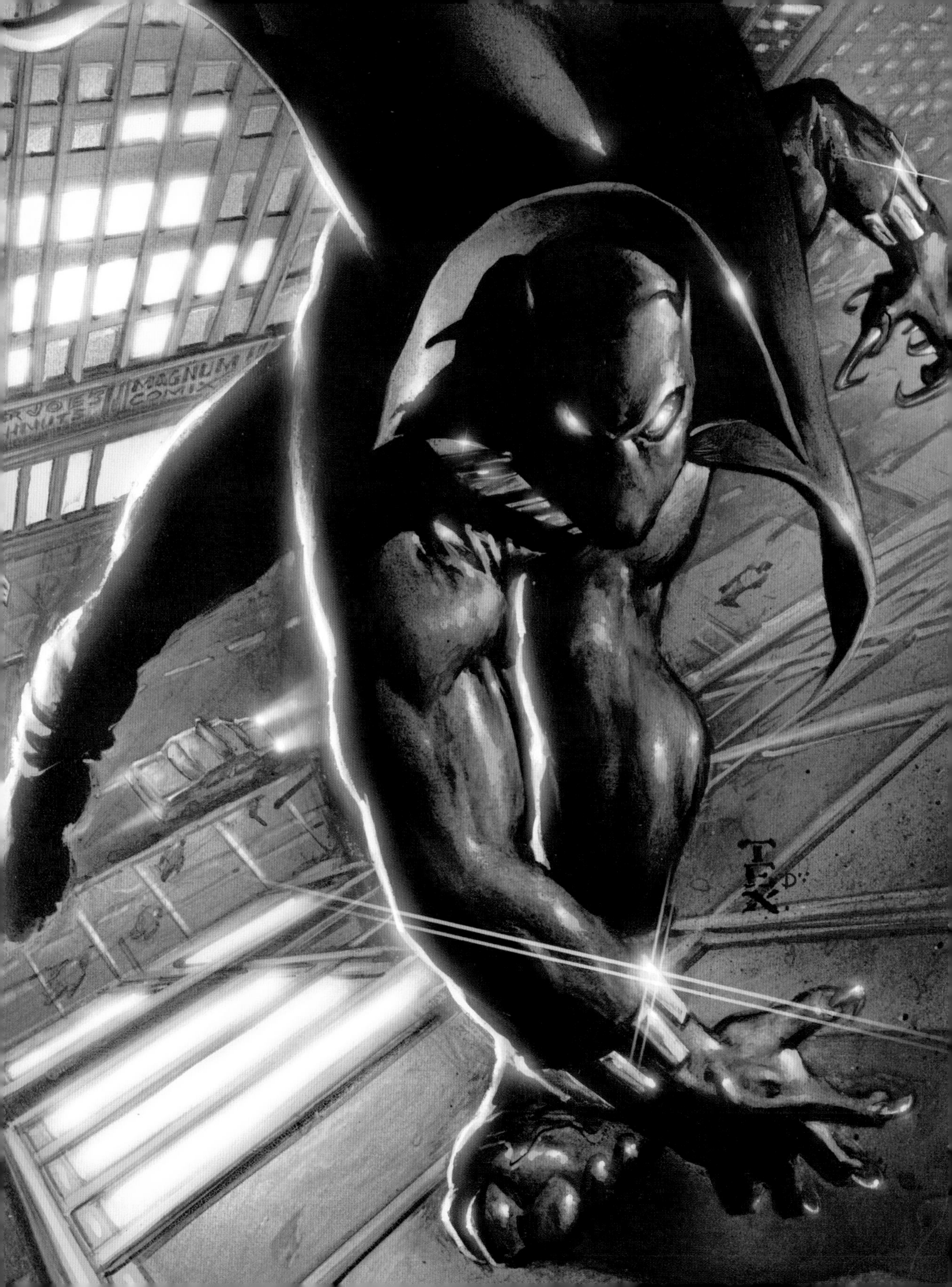
JOE'S
MAGNUM COMIX

MEET THE COSPLAYER:

★ ★ EVERYBODY LOVES TONY RAY! ★ ★

THERE IS ALWAYS ONE COSPLAYER AT EVERY CONVEN-tion who is usually at the front of a group cosplay gathering, maybe organizing the shoot itself, or even volunteering at the Marvel booth. And for as long as I've been attending comic conventions, Tony Ray has always been one of *those* cosplayers, greeting you with a smiling face. Which all makes sense because he first dipped his toe into cosplay all the way back in 1999, when he was the chief science officer of his high school's science fiction club. Although he was early to join the fandom, it wasn't until later, in 2007, that he fully embraced the community, after seeing fellow cosplayers at local conventions.

Born and raised in the Bronx, he recalls, "I was lucky enough to have been taught how to use a sewing machine thanks to my grandmother. So, I had the basic skills, and with them just started making things I wanted, a costume coat here, a full bodysuit there, but if there was ever something that I didn't know how to do I would turn to the internet and take the time to learn the new skill. From there I could make the ideas I had on paper become a real thing." And he has certainly spent the last twenty-plus years bringing a plethora of Marvel characters from the comic panel, or screen, to life.

Starting with Bishop from the X-Men as his first Marvel cosplay, Tony has since cosplayed Cyclops, Patriot, Storm, Black Panther, Tony Stark, Spider-Man, Killmonger, Cloak, and more. He has also encouraged fellow fans to create their first cosplays, especially advocating for people of color to find a place within the cosplay community. The Wakanda and Black Panther cosplay meetups at Dragon Con each year are so much fun to attend, as the sounds of *yibambe, yibambe* echo across the patio.

Thus, the Black Panther is a very familiar build for

Tony, as he has done countless versions of T'Challa from comics, films, and games. So when a new design was announced for Eve L. Ewing and Chris Allen's 2023 comic series, he knew he had to make it. "It was the accessories for this costume that drew me in. The spear and daggers looked like they would be a fun inspiration to design and build."

With the challenge set, join Tony as he takes you step by step to build your own Black Panther cosplay inspired by the new comic!

MAKING OF

★ ★ THE BLACK PANTHER ★ ★

COSPLAY BUILD NOTES

IN THIS FINAL PROJECT, YOU'LL BE COMBINING ALL THE skills you've learned in this book to craft a Black Panther suit, its accessories (scarf, thigh holster, and chest harness), as well as his shield and weapons. This build combines a variety of techniques, including sewing, foam work, and 3D printing. For the helmet piece of the suit, we chose to commission one from a fellow cosplayer because it is a more complex build, but you can also purchase one from a Marvel licensee like Hasbro if you'd like.

Since Black Panther's suit is similar to a catsuit, we aimed to recreate that sleek design with the use of spandex for the base, but another option is to use an alternative stretchable material or even a denser fabric like pleather to resemble armor. To build the shape of the suit, we'll be using a dress form to sketch out the lines and shapes, then using plastic wrap and duct tape (similar to what we did with Ironheart in Chapter 7) to create rough pattern pieces. (Dress forms come in various sizes: choose one that matches your body size.) Another option is to adapt a pre-bought or homemade bodysuit, similar to the process for Captain America in chapter 5, to build out the pattern. Then to create the shield, we will be using EVA foam, while the daggers, as well as the spear point and heel, will be assembled as 3D-printed objects.

With a bit of post-production magic, Tony as T'challa and By The Goddess as Storm pose in Wakanda.

"Before the premiere of *Black Panther*, from just a few shots in the trailer, I decided to make one of T'Challa's outfits. At SDCC later that summer, I got to meet and get autographs from Chadwick Boseman, Letitia Wright, and Winston Duke all while wearing the costume. A dream come true for a fan!"

—Tony Ray

MATERIALS

SUPER SUIT

- Plastic wrap
- Duct tape
- 3 to 4 yards of black spandex
- 2 to 3 yards of scrap spandex (optional)
- Black thread
- 22- to 24-inch black zipper
- Hook and eye (optional)

SUIT ACCESSORIES (CHEST HARNESS, THIGH HOLSTER, AND SCARF)

- 1 yard of brown pleather
- 6½-inch rare earth magnets
- 8 silver 6mm rivets
- Contact cement or super glue
- 3 medium leather closures with silver buckles
- 1 large snap
- 2 to 3 yards white fabric

3D-PRINTED SPEAR AND DAGGERS

- 3D modeling software or print-ready files
- 3D printer and PLA plastic filament
- Epoxy or other 3D-print-friendly glue
- Range of sandpaper from 60 to 320 grit
- Sandable spray filler-primer
- Spray or acrylic paint in white and silver
- 1¼-inch diameter staff (PVC or wood), adjusted for your height
- Wood stain

SHIELD

- 1 sheet of 4mm EVA foam
- Plasti Dip or alternate foam primer
- Spray or acrylic paint in black
- Acrylic paint in blue, red, yellow, orange, and white
- Clear matte acrylic sealant or matte varnish
- 10- to 12-inch-long narrow dowel (PVC or wood)
- ½ yard of 1-inch-wide elastic

PURCHASED ITEMS

- Helmet
- Black tabi shoes

ADDITIONAL SEWING AND CRAFTING ITEMS

- 3D printer with any added tools
- Chalk
- Colored markers
- Craft knife or blade
- Dress form
- Heat gun or hair dryer
- Iron, ironing board, and pressing cloth
- Pattern paper
- Pins
- Rivet tools including hole punch and rivet punch
- Ruler
- Scissors
- Scotch tape
- Sewing machine, with zipper foot

BUILDING THE SUPER SUIT PATTERN

1. Start by using a dress form as the base, add a layer of plastic wrap covering either the left or right side of the form, and then a layer of duct tape over it. As we'll be mirroring the pattern, we'll only be using one half of the form.

2. Sketch out the design of the suit including the front, back, side, and sleeve.

3. Carefully remove the duct tape shape from the dress form and cut out each pattern piece.

4. Transfer each piece onto pattern paper, smoothing out any rough lines or curves, then with a ruler add a ½-inch seam allowance for each piece.

5. Label and copy over any final notes and notches on your patterns, then cut out one of each of the pattern pieces:
   - Front
   - Back
   - Waist including leg
   - Sleeve

TIP: Even if you have extra fabric, it is always a good idea to plan out how each pattern will fit on the fabric, taking stretch and bias into consideration.

6. Lay each pattern piece down on the black spandex fabric, right side down, and mark out the following:
   - 1 front (cut on the fold)
   - 2 back—cut two
   - 2 waist—cut two
   - 2 sleeves—cut two

7. Transfer any lines and notches onto the fabric, then cut out all your pieces.

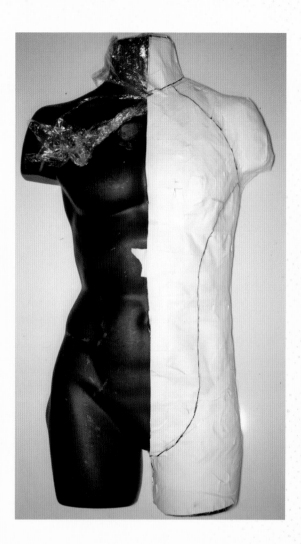

1. Starting with right sides together, pin the front piece to the left waist piece at the side seams, then sew together. Repeat with the right waist piece.

TIP: When using stretch fabric, use a zigzag stitch; if you have access to a serger, it is a great way to stitch a spandex bodysuit together.

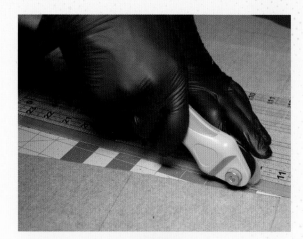

2. Next, starting with the left sleeve, with right sides facing, align the front shoulder edge to the corresponding edge on the front and side, pin, and then sew. Then follow this process for the back of the sleeve and top seam. Repeat for the right sleeve.

3. For the back, pin and then sew the left side to the left back. Repeat for the right side back.

4. Next, for the legs, right sides facing, pin the inside seams together, from the bottom of the left leg to the center crotch seams and then back down to the bottom of the right leg, then stitch them together.

TIP: When sewing high-stress areas like the crotch of the pants, you may want to pass over the area a second, or even third, time with your machine to ensure your seam is secure and prevent any costume malfunctions.

5. To prep the back seam for the zipper, pin and sew the back seam from the inside leg seam to the notch that indicates the end of the zipper.

6. Now check the bodysuit fit and adjust or add any seams as needed.

   Now, we'll start adding in the details to finish the suit, starting with the collar.

7. First measure the collar length. Then cut a strip of your suit material that is 3 inches wide and the collar length plus 2 inches.

8. Fold the fabric strip horizontally, wrong sides together, pin, and then stitch it to the collar of the bodysuit.

   Next, you'll install the zipper.

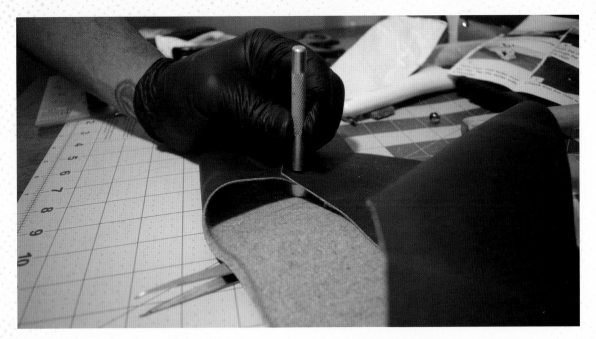

9. Starting with the left side of the suit, pin, and using your zipper foot, stitch it onto the bodysuit. Repeat with the left side of the zipper.

10. As an optional addition, you can hand-sew a hook and eye to the top of the back collar above the zipper.

11. Test the fit and then finish the wrist and ankle raw edges to your liking.

Last, we'll create a set of gloves.

12. Fold some black spandex in half, with the right sides together. Place your hand down onto the wrong side of the fabric, and then trace the shape of your hand, wrist, and forearm, spreading your fingers, to leave a ½-inch gap between each finger.

13. Pin along the outline and then stitch.

14. Test the fit and then cut and trim the excess fabric around the seam.

15. Turn the glove right side out, test the fit once more, and then finish the edge.

BUILDING THE SUIT ACCESSORIES

Now we'll make the straps for the chest harness, thigh hostler, and shoulder harness.

1. For the chest harness and thigh holster, measure the length needed for each strap by measuring the circumference of your chest and thigh.

2. Lay the brown pleather fabric out, right side down. Using a ruler, draw out the shapes needed for the different pieces and straps, adding ½-inch seam allowance to all sides.

TIP: As you measure out each piece, remember to keep in mind how you're planning to put each on and then take it off.

3. There are three different straps for the shoulder harness: the wide main strap, a thinner and longer strap to connect the harness, and then a final thinner strap for the daggers. Draw out one of each of these shapes, with corresponding lengths:

- The main strap measured 2½ inches wide.
- The cross strap measured 1 inch wide.
- The dagger strap measured ½ inch wide.

For the thigh holster pouches, there will be three pieces for each pouch: one long wraparound center and two sides.

1. First, determine how tall and wide you'd like each pouch to be. For this build, we decided on 6 inches tall by 3 inches wide and 1 inch deep.
2. Measure and draw out two center pieces that are 18 inches tall by 3 inches wide, then add a ½-inch seam allowance.
3. Measure and draw out four side pieces measuring 6 inches tall by 1 inch wide, then add a ½-inch seam allowance.
4. Measure and draw two straps at 1 inch wide and corresponding length.
5. Then cut out each of the measured shapes and straps.

TIP: You can also purchase pre-made pouches online, and match them to your costume using some fabric paint.

Now, we will assemble the thigh holster.

6. Starting with right sides together, pin and sew the left-side pieces of the pouch to the center piece at the front and then the back. Repeat with the right-side pieces.

TIP: For cleaner corners, you can trim and glue down any excess fabric.

7. Turn right side out and finish the seam edge of the pouch's flap.
8. Glue the positive side of a magnet to the inside of the pouch, and match with the negative side glued to the underside of the flap.
9. Repeat for the second pouch.
10. Finish the edges of the two straps as desired, then attach the buckle closures to each strap.

Finally, we'll assemble the straps into the different elements. Finish the edges of each strap. You can use a topstitch or paint to add detailing.

For the main strap, we'll be securing it in a loop around your shoulder with rivets, but you can stitch or glue it closed if you'd like.

11. Measure and draw where the two rivets will go at the ends of the strap.
12. Punch the necessary holes into the fabric using a pair of punching pliers or a hole punch.
13. Attach the rivets to the strap.

Next, we'll attach the cross strap to the main strap, with the buckle closure at the back.

14. For the front, attach the end of the strap to the main strap using two rivets, following the steps above.
15. Then on the back, following the above steps, rivet one end of the buckle closure to the main strap, and the other to the end of the strap.

The final strap is how we will attach the 3D-printed daggers to the harness.

16. Secure each end of the final strap to the cross strap using the final two rivets, following the process above.
17. Then measure where the four daggers will go and glue the positive side of a magnet to the back side of the strap. The connecting side of the magnet will be attached to the daggers below.
18. To prevent the harness from shifting, attach one side of a large snap to the underside of the top of the shoulder. The corresponding side of the snap will then go on the right side of the super suit.

1. Draft out the shape and size for the shield on a piece of pattern paper, using a mirror to adjust the length and width, dependent on your body shape. Then cut out the pattern.
2. Transfer the pattern to a sheet of 4mm EVA foam.
3. With a sharp craft knife or blade, cut out the shape.
4. Using a heat gun or hair dryer, shape the curve of the shield.
5. Once it has cooled, add a layer of primer to the front of the shield, then a layer of black spray paint.
6. Next, draft the design onto the shield.
7. Using the acrylic paints, hand-paint the design onto the shield, then finish with a clear coat of sealant.

TIP: Use different colors and brushstrokes to create detail and texture when painting, such as distressing to give it a weathered, battle-damaged look.

8. To add support, attach the short dowel vertically to the center line on the back of the shield with glue.
9. Finally, measure the circumference of your biceps and cut out the needed length of the elastic. Glue each end to the back of the shield.

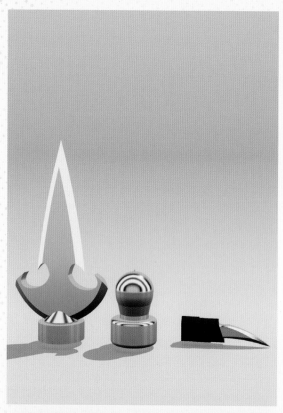

1. Using existing templates, draft out the digital versions of the accessories using 3D modeling software. You'll be printing the below pieces:
   - 1 spear point
   - 1 spear heel
   - 4 daggers
2. Export each 3D model as a watertight .stl file and load it into your 3D printer's software to slice, support, and prepare the model for print.

TIP: Head over to our Loki chapter for a deeper dive into the different types of 3D printers and the process of modeling and finishing pieces.

3. After the prints have finished, sand down any rough edges, and if needed, you can use a primer to fill in any gaps.
4. Prep each piece for painting with a layer of primer and then white spray paint.

   We'll then paint and assemble each element.

SPEAR

1. For both the point and heel of the spear, add a layer of metallic silver spray paint.
2. Then add a layer of high-gloss clear spray paint.
3. Finish the dowel using a wood stain of your choice.
4. After the paint and stain have dried, attach the point and heel to each side of the dowel using an epoxy or other 3D-print-friendly glue.

TIP: When posing with props, like a spear with 3D-printed pieces, remember to take extra care as you'll likely want it to last a few wearings.

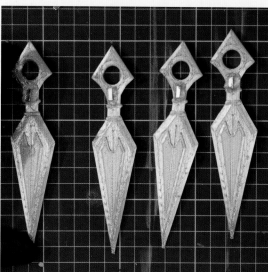

DAGGERS

1. Follow the steps above from the spear pieces to paint and seal each dagger.
2. Glue the negative side of a rare earth magnet to the back of each dagger.
3. Once the glue has dried, test out the magnet connection by attaching to the chest strap.

THE FINAL LOOK

Finishing the costume with a piece of white fabric to drape around your neck for the scarf and the helmet, give yourself a pat on the back for continuing to build your crafting skills. Take the time to see how each element feels and adjust if needed. Then take up your spear and strike a pose, as you're ready to ascend to claim the throne of Wakanda!

PART III

GET READY FOR YOUR DEBUT!

★ ★ ★

CHAPTER 10

Finishing Touches to Bring Your Cosplay to Life

Embellishments, shoes, wigs, makeup: these are just a few of the extra details you can add to your now brand-new cosplay. Although not necessarily required, each will add a little shine and a different level of completion.

★ ★ ADDING A PERSONAL TOUCH WITH EMBELLISHMENTS ★ ★

EVERY COSPLAYER ADDS SOMETHING FROM THEIR own personal style to each costume. With how long I've been in the community, it's become my habit to be able to spot a specific cosplayer from across the convention floor, either from their immaculate wig skills, the intricate embroidery, or even the beautiful paint job.

That said, now is the perfect time to dive into how you can add your own personal embellishments to your cosplay. These touches could be in the fabric you choose, as you saw with the blue scale material Mark used on his Captain America top, or with Indra, who chose a shimmering red metallic spandex for her Phoenix suit.

Or you could take a trip into the magical world of trims. At your local fabric store, there is usually a whole aisle dedicated to by-the-yard trim options, such as fringe, braid, and piping. Fringe may not necessarily make sense for your super suit, but adding piping or bias detailing can add that extra *pop* to break up a one-color suit—that's exactly how both Raisa and Marc used gold bias to finish the edges of their two costumes.

Lauren St. Laurent pairs her embellished cosplay with a wig.

Using a wide variety of gold trim Dessi-Desu brings her Art Deco Loki illustration to life.

things to do once you set up your new machine is to test out the stitches, so you can see what each will look like, playing with the stitch length and widths. There just might be one that will be perfect for your current cosplay. Adding a decorative stitch is also a great way to add dimension to your leather straps, any fabric coverings, and finished seams.

Stitching is also the best way to add those iconic emblems on super suits like the star on Mark's Captain America shirt or the lightning bolt on Raisa's Ms. Marvel. Appliqué can be a bit tricky, especially when you start working with more complex designs, but a good way to add a level of polish and detail to your cosplays.

Going hand in hand with appliqué is embroidery. This is a skill that many cosplayers use to add unique details and really add that personal touch to their work. If you are worried about doing things the old-fashioned way, don't be! There are specialty sewing machines, including stand-alone embroidery machines, that allow you to upload specific stitches and designs digitally and then stitch them without you having to pick up a needle. And if you aren't ready to buy a fancy machine, you can always buy or commission custom iron-on embroidered patches, which is what we used for the opening of the *Marvel Becoming* videos.

The final two options for embellishments are beading and distressing; both add a personal touch to your work and allow you to show off your crafting skills. With extensive options, beads are available in plastic, glass, stone, shell, and pearl. And you can go from single beads to adding an elaborate beaded design, or even increasing the sparkle factor with rhinestones or sequins.

Distressing has been around for as long as there have been costumes and it is certainly its own unique art. Most costuming crews on film and TV sets have a breakdown artist on payroll to specifically distress the clothes seen on screen. The technique is when you

You could even use what you have on hand to create your own trims and embellishments. This can be anything from homemade bias tape to braiding strips to create your own cording, or using feathers, beads, or lace you have lying around in your craft room. Creating your own trim using leftover fabric and scraps is great for the wallet and also a sustainable option so you aren't just throwing one more thing in the trash. If you're interested in exploring this, head online as there are a wide range of tutorials to start you off.

Another easy way to add details is through decorative stitching, either with a standard topstitch, hand embroidery, or by exploring the different stitches that may be built into your sewing machine. Higher end machines will usually have a larger collection, but even the entry-level machines will have a good selection for you to work with. One of the best use different tools, from tea baths to burning, to give your costume a weathered, aged look. Acrylic paints are a great tool to add that edge to armor, props, and even fabric.

For your first costume, you may want to keep things simple, or you might not need to use all the techniques explored in this chapter, but with each new cosplay comes a new opportunity to learn and expand your library of skills.

CLICK YOUR HEELS TOGETHER . . .

SHOES MIGHT BE ON THE BOTTOM, LITERALLY, OF YOUR to-do list, but the goal is always to match what works best for your cosplay, along with being practical and comfortable to wear. Now if this costume is just for a photo shoot or party, you have the option to be a little more frivolous. But if you're planning to walk for hours at a convention, comfort is a great thing to keep in mind. So maybe think twice about wearing a pair of high heels if they are not your normal go-to, or at least plan to bring a pair of comfy flats with you for the walking and standing parts of the day.

When deciding on shoes, there are a few options, from purchasing a new pair, reusing a pair you already own, or building a boot cover. What you choose will depend on the planned final look of the costume, and how closely you want to match the original design.

The easiest route is to find a pair of shoes or boots you already have in your closet. It's nice on the wallet, while giving you peace of mind knowing how they fit. But if that's not an option, it's time to start searching. You'll be surprised what you can find at thrift stores or online; I've found some great shoes for past cosplays thanks to Amazon and eBay. With some love, attention, and some leather paint, an old pair of shoes can look fresh and also match the colors of your costume.

Bright blue high-top Converse go perfectly with Cyberbird's version of the Kotobukiya bishoujo Jubilee.

For more intricate cosplays, you may want to make boot covers. Despite what you might think, it is very, very rare for a cosplayer to build their own shoes from scratch. Boot covers allow cosplayers to have that unique shoe by building a structure, with fabric and sometimes foam, that goes around existing shoes or

125

boots. These can be tricky builds and might rely on a little trial and error, but thankfully there are a few patterns available that can be used to start off with. Just as with your costume, the best bet is to start with a mock-up, so you can test out how to fit your shoes, and how it feels to walk in them. I've actually built multiple boot covers over one pair of shoes using the same pattern, which was a great help because I had less to pack and bring to conventions. And don't forget that foam is a great way to add detail or even help keep the shape and form—it's not just for building armor!

Shoes can easily eat into your budget and timeline, so take the time early on to plan out what you're wearing. And if you can, take a few walks around your apartment to feel them out. Every cosplayer has accidentally worn a pair of shoes that turned out to be a struggle on the con floor, so don't worry if you opt for comfort or low cost over style.

★ ★ GO WIG OR GO HOME ★ ★

Hooked On Phoenix pairs a dark green wig with body paint for her She-Hulk cosplay.

WE'VE FINALLY COME TO ONE OF THE MOST ICONIC tools in a cosplayer's arsenal: *wigs*. Hair and its styling have been an aspect of status throughout human history; we have records of wigs being used going all the way back to 3400 BC in ancient Egypt. And we've all heard the stories of Marie Antoinette's pompadour and the white powder wigs of America's founders. From the start, wigs have been a part of showcasing fashion trends, voicing political statements, or a necessary tool at center stage. Up until the last few decades, the only wig options were human or animal hair, but now with the introduction of different synthetic materials, wigs have become affordable and thus more accessible.

Synthetic wigs have expanded the options for style, color, and quality since those early days of Halloween costume wigs. From larger online retailers to smaller cosplay wig companies, such as Arda Wigs and Epic Cosplay Wigs, you can now purchase specific colors and designs, even pre-styled, for the current hot character or series. Gone are the days when you had to use permanent marker to make a dye bath for your wig; now you have a wide variety of shades to choose from, including that perfect dark green for She-Hulk. When you're deciding on a color, you'll want to find one that matches the character, but also keep your own skin

Wig stylist Vickie Bane in her 1990s Storm cosplay.

tone in mind. Depending on whether you have either a warm or cool skin tone, some wig colors may just be more complementary than others.

Along with the wide range of colors, you also have the choice of hard front or lace front wigs. If a wig has bangs, either short, long, or side-swept, the wig would be classified as a hard front. These are the standard option when looking for wigs, as they tend to be the least expensive. For your first wig, a hard front is the perfect choice, as they come in the biggest variety of colors and styles and are the easiest to wear. However, if you're looking for a more realistic hairline at your forehead, then you may want to choose a lace front wig. As it says on the label, lace front wigs have a piece of lace sewn into the front of the wig, which allows you to manipulate the hairline and glue it down to your forehead.

With a little makeup, the wig will fade into your natural hairline and can appear just like your actual hair. Also, the glue, or wig tape, provides an additional level of security to make sure the wig stays on your head. One thing to keep in mind is that lace front wigs tend to be higher in price and are likely to be available in a smaller selection of colors and styles.

On top of the large variety of wigs, there are also now wig accessories like clip-in ponytails, braids, or bangs. These can be an easy solution for a character with a ponytail or to add hair styling if you plan to use your own hair. I did this recently for a non-Marvel character, using my actual hair to style a hair bump, then adding a ponytail extension.

Unless you've commissioned a fully pre-styled wig, before you get to the convention, you'll likely have to take that wig out of the bag and give it a comb and a

127

style. Yes, there are wigs you can take straight out of the bag, ready to wear, but I always like to give a wig a little love before slamming it on my head. Below is a list of basic tools to have on hand when working with a wig:

WIG HEAD

Along with a wig stand, together they'll allow you to work on a wig without having to wear it. (Sometimes the stand and head are one unit.) You'll want to use a few of those straight pins from your sewing toolbox to make sure the wig stays on the Styrofoam head. And when you venture into further styling, wig heads are a great way to store and travel with styled wigs.

WhoaChrisWhoa shows off his wig skills for his Spider-Punk cosplay at AnimeExpo.

CUTTING TOOLS

A good pair of scissors you already have can work for trimming and cutting hair, but if you're looking for a softer look, you may also want to pick up a pair of hair cutting shears.

COMBS

As your wig is not made to be brushed like your hair, you'll want to pick up a comb to detangle your wig and give it a fresh look. There are also wig-specific combs and brushes that you can purchase.

HAIR SPRAY

Use it exactly how you use it for your own hair! But don't be afraid to use as much hair spray and gel as your wig may need, as it's made for you to do so. In this instance, more is usually better. Plus, it's always a good idea to have a small can packed in your cosplay kit.

Beyond basic styling, there are many ways you can manipulate a wig, especially with a synthetic fiber wig. One easy styling method is to combine two wigs by removing the wefts—basically a line of hair sewn together—from one wig and hand-sewing it into the second wig. This can give your wig a fuller or longer look, or even add additional color. If you have a heat-resistant wig, another option is to use heat-based tools to curl, straighten, or add in some crazy spikes. One thing I've learned over the years is that there is no limit on how far you can take a wig. Just take one look at *Marvel Becoming*'s Vickie Bane's Instagram (@vickiebane) feed to see the incredible wigs she styles. Thankfully, most Marvel characters tend to go with a more natural look!

Once you're ready to wear your wig, you'll want to make sure you have the right accessory to keep that wig on your head. Depending on the length and thickness of your hair, you'll likely want to braid and flatten your hair to your head before pulling on a wig cap. Here are a few additional items to use to keep that wig secured to your head.

WIG CAP

The basic tool for creating a foundation for your wig. Wig caps come in a variety of styles and colors. I prefer a mesh version, especially with my short hair, as it creates additional places to pin the wig down.

WIG GRIP

Worn like a headband, this is a newer option on the market that creates a stable base to help prevent the wig from slipping back on your head.

BOBBY PINS

Likely you have a few in your house already, but these are a must to anchor the wig on your head. And don't skimp when adding them, as the more you use, the more secure your wig will be.

WIG GLUE OR TAPE

Specifically for lace front (and full lace) wigs, wig glue or tape is needed for creating that natural-looking hairline. There are a few wig glue options available, but eyelash glue also works in a pinch.

At the end of the day, deciding what to choose depends on your character, budget, and comfort level working with a wig. It can be as simple as using your natural hair or splurging for a human hair wig. There is no right answer, just what makes sense for you.

Dax Exclamationpoint pairs makeup with a stylized wig for her She-Hulk cosplay.

★ ★ BUILDING YOUR COSPLAY MAKEUP KIT ★ ★

AS COSPLAY HAS GROWN AND EXPANDED, SO HAS THE makeup we all use. In the early days, my friends and I barely wore foundation, let alone primer. And certainly, wearing makeup is not required, but it is one of the ways to add a little fun and sparkle to your final look—especially with the sheer number of options available at your nearby makeup store. At conventions, I love discovering a new product when I'm huddled in front of the mirror with my friends getting into cosplay.

And here is your friendly reminder to wear sunscreen: it's always a good idea to make it part of your skin routine before applying makeup. Also, I know the feeling of coming back from a long day at a convention

129

When choosing a wig, find one that works best for you, as Evil Clever Dog demonstrates in her Kamala cosplay.

Every cosplayer adds something from their own personal style to each costume.

and just diving into bed. But before you do, take the time to take off those eyelashes, clean your contacts, and wash your face. Your skin will thank you later!

The industry is always evolving; I'm going to lay out the current products I keep packed in my cosplay kit, plus a few tips and tricks to keep in mind.

PRIMER

The first step for makeup application, primers create a buildable base for foundation and eyeshadow and help it stay longer. Eyeshadow primer has been a game changer for me, especially when applying bright colors to keep them looking great all day.

FOUNDATION AND CONCEALER

Matching your skin tone, foundation is the first layer for your face, while concealer can be used for additional coverage to specific areas like under your eyes or to hide blemishes. There are a vast range of foundation brands, coverages, and formulas; try a few to find which works best for you.

CONTOURING

A modern trend, contouring is achieved by using dark and light shades to enhance certain facial features. Although a more advanced skill, contouring is certainly useful in cosplay makeup, especially if you're looking to shift the appearance of your age or gender.

BLUSH AND HIGHLIGHTER

Blush has been used for thousands of years, but it is still a great esthetic, adding that flush of color to your cheeks. You can use the color to match your cosplay: use a pinker, brighter tone for that princess look, while a darker, elegant color creates an evening look. And used along with blush, highlighter can add a glow to your cheeks, while accentuating your bone structure. I love adding a hint of gold shimmer to all my makeup looks!

EYESHADOW

Available in the full spectrum of the rainbow, eyeshadow is the paint palette for your face. From a more natural, subdued look to that added pop of color, eyeshadow is where you tell the story of your character with makeup. It's my favorite tool in the kit, and what I typically will spend the most time on.

Cosplayer Dade Elza poses on set of *Marvel Becoming* in a prosthetic Skrull mask built by Keaghlan Ashley.

EYELINER

Since the time of the Egyptians, eyeliner has been used to enhance and shape the eye. Available in a wide range of colors, it's most commonly seen in black and brown. With cosplay, you can use eyeliner to create an intense look that will help define your eyes in photos.

MASCARA AND EYELASHES

Along with eyeliner, mascara is used to augment your eyes by darkening, thickening, and lengthening your eyelashes. Together with fake eyelashes, it's a game changer, adding drama to your makeup, and further "opening" your eyes for photos. When looking to purchase fake eyelashes, choose the shape that works best for your costume, and don't forget the glue to attach them, being sure it's safe for eyes!

EYEBROW ENHANCEMENTS

Not a specific tool, but you do not want to forget about your eyebrows, either using brow gel, brow pen or pencil, or even a pomade. Each gives you the ability to structure your eyebrow shape, from thickening or thinning to adding a villainous detail or even matching the color of your wig.

LIPSTICK

Not always necessary, but lipstick can complete your color palette. A bright red can easily match your sash detail, or a simple gloss can help convey a more natural look.

SETTING SPRAY

The final tool for all makeup looks! A setting spray will literally help seal in the makeup to last all day, and even through the night.

You can certainly add and subtract items dependent on your personal preferences and as you learn different makeup techniques, especially if you're looking for a different esthetic, such as spooky or if you're going the body paint route.

Milly Cosplay blends body paint and a long-sleeved bodysuit to create her Nebula look.

There are a wide variety of different paints and tools that you can use for a full-body look, from airbrush to crème based. As I've done a few blue versions of Mystique, personally I prefer a water-based makeup as it's easier to apply and clean off and is less harsh for your skin. There is also the option of airbrush makeup, but it can be time consuming depending on the amount of skin to cover. If aiming for a more intricate look for a convention or a photo shoot, you can book a makeup artist to assist. There is also the choice of purchasing a similar-colored bodysuit, gloves, and leggings to wear underneath a costume, which will remove the need to paint so much skin. Easier to clean up, too!

133

Minakess poses in her Kitty Pryde cosplay with the best companion, Lockheed.

colors. Fake blood can be whipped up at home with standard ingredients from your closet, like corn syrup, red food coloring, and flour. And a scar can be added using a scarring liquid like Rigid Collodion. If you want more, there is the expansive world of special effects makeup including bald caps, prosthetics, and latex.

As you plan the look for your upcoming cosplay, here are a few tips to keep in mind. Again, sunscreen is your skin's best friend, along with washing the makeup off after a long day. Also, keep an eye on the day's weather, as if it's going to be incredibly hot and humid, or a rainy day, you'll want to adjust your plan for makeup, including using waterproof or sweat-proof makeup, along with an extra layer of setting spray. Finally, makeup does not last forever, and all products do have an expiration date. For example, mascara should be replaced every six months or so. As you're applying most of these on your face and near your eyes, when possible, look to purchase a new one.

It's easy to see that for makeup, the options are really limitless. I'll leave you with one final note: makeup can be used by anyone. Just like actors on stage or screen, makeup can be used for all genders to enhance facial structures and create smoothness for photos. It's just one more tool for you to use as a cosplayer.

If you're looking to be a little more adventurous, maybe you'll want to add a fake scar or blood to make your cosplay feel a little more rough and dangerous. Learning special effects makeup can be an advanced skill but it is certainly a lot of fun to try, and it adds an extra element to your final cosplay. For bruising, you can pick up a bruise wheel palette or even use some eyeshadow, and with a sponge build on the moody

★ ★ THE FINAL DETAILS ★ ★

AS YOU PREPARE FOR A COSPLAY NIGHT OUT, HERE are few additional ideas to think about as you finalize your costume:

CONTACTS

Either to help you see, or to adjust the color of your eyes, contact lenses are a fun accessory. And they certainly can earn you a double take, like when I wear my yellow contacts for Mystique.

JEWELRY

From large hoop earrings for your America Chavez costume to a classy pearl necklace for a 1940s Agent Carter, jewelry can elevate the final look.

134

Cosplay couple Allen Hansard and Mary Hansard-Cahela met through cosplay before marrying in 2018.

NAIL POLISH AND PRESS-ON NAILS

Crafting can do a number on your hands and nails, so a new coat of nail polish, or even press-on nails, can give your hands a fresh look. Match your character with a green for your She-Hulk cosplay, or some fake claws as Sabretooth.

SHAPEWEAR

A foundation garment, shapewear is an undergarment that helps smooth your figure. It's incredibly helpful when you are wearing anything made with spandex, especially a super suit. Worn under your cosplay, shapewear is available in a wide variety of shapes, sizes, and for use on the different areas of your body. Options include a bodysuit to smooth out curves, a binder to create a more masculine shape, or a dancer belt to provide a special kind of support.

TIGHTS

Along with shapewear, tights are base layers you should always consider when thinking of certain cosplays, like Psylocke's leotard. At a slightly higher price, dancer tights are a great option, giving you uniform coverage, especially in photos, while still being breathable. Plus, they tend to be sturdier for repeated use.

PROPS

In addition to any iconic props you've crafted or purchased, from Captain America's shield or Thor's hammer, you can always add an extra accessory. Maybe it's an Infinity Stone, a Chewie cat plushy, or even a custom "The Mary Janes" record. A prop can show off your creativity and be a talking point when meeting new friends.

★ ★ SERIOUSLY, THE FINAL-FINAL STEP ★ ★

I'VE WALKED YOU THROUGH THE MANY, MANY STEPS IN sewing and crafting a cosplay. From learning fabric to working with foam, each chapter has, I hope, brought you to this moment, where you're ready to show off your brand-new costume to the world. And in the next chapter, I'll walk you through how to do that, from conventions to competitions and photo shoots. But before that, there are a few final things to check off, and I swear these are the final build tips and tricks I'll pass along.

Cosplay can be a family activity as Brett Yee's children join him in their Shang-Chi costumes.

On every cosplayer's to-do list before debuting a cosplay is the test wear. Basically, it's time to put on each layer—shapewear, costume pieces, armor, wig, shoes, etc.—and ask yourself a few questions: Do the items all fit together? Can you walk easily enough? Do you need a handler? Where will your wallet and phone go?

Besides helping you get an idea of how much time you'll need to get ready, it will also help you notice any last-minute fixes needed, while giving you an idea of what it feels like wearing it all together. In the past, I've made the mistake of not doing this, and then I've had to scramble to glue and paint while getting ready in the hotel room. Not a fun experience! Along with a test fit, if you have the time, plan for a makeup trial, especially if it's a new look or tool you're using, such as your first time doing body paint.

Once in costume, step in front of your mirror, and take a moment to think about the poses you can have planned for when asked for a photo. Maybe it's the iconic Spider-Man *thwip* or Black Widow's landing pose, but you'll want a few poses in mind so you're not fumbling in the moment at the convention. Plus, with the mirror, you can see what the costume and pose looks like on your body. And if you have a prop, play with it to see what it can add to a pose, or the limitations of your movement with the prop. One more cosplay-mom moment: keeping safety in mind, it's never a good idea to swing or throw your prop unless you're in a controlled environment.

Finally, grab a selfie of yourself, as it's time to share with your friends and community that you've finished your first cosplay. The hard part is over, and now it's time to share your creation with the world!

CHAPTER 11

Going Out into the World

It's finally that magical time to present your brand-spanking-new cosplay to the world. For the last chapter, let's walk you through debuting your new costume, advice for first-time convention attendees, social media, and finally, how to pack and store your costume until the next event.

★ ★ IT'S YOUR CONVENTION 101 ★ ★

CONVENTIONS HAVE COME VERY FAR FROM THOSE early science fiction cons in the 1930s. Now there are events for every type of fandom, from coast to coast, and on almost every continent. Maybe even by this printing there will be one on Antarctica. It may seem a little intimidating to attend your first convention in costume, but with a few tips under your utility belt you'll be ready to strut and pose on the convention floor.

To start off, you'll want to nail down any event logistics—travel, hotel, and badge. Even if it's a local convention, lock down the plan for travel, especially if you need to purchase airplane or train tickets. With your credit card already out, make sure you've secured a hotel for the weekend. If you're only attending for a day, a hotel room may not be required, but something to think about is how and when you're getting into costume, and then later out of it. Many cosplayers have driven or taken public transportation in costume to a convention. Most New Yorkers know it's Comic Con weekend when you're riding the subway next to a Deadpool. But, for major shows, a hotel can be a requirement, especially if you're planning to bring a larger cosplay. A whole other book could be written about the process that goes into securing a hotel room

for the bigger shows, like San Diego Comic-Con and Dragon Con. Without going too deep into it all, aim to think far ahead, and look to join fan-run groups on social media for guidance.

For some shows, badges can also be tricky to acquire, but most conventions allow same-day purchase of either weekend or one-day badges.

With the con logistics settled, next up is to plan out your cosplay schedule and decide when you're wearing what. This can always evolve once you arrive, but it's good to have a strategy, especially if you're looking to attend a meetup or have scheduled time with a photographer. Your convention plans, the weather, scheduled photo shoots, and more will help you determine when the best time is for you to assemble your cosplay. And no matter how many times you'll put on a costume, it always ends up taking longer than you planned for on the day, so it's always good to pad your schedule. With that in mind, make sure to also allow time for food, water, and rest, because not all costumes can be worn for long periods of time, and it may not be easy to eat or drink in costume.

As your plan comes together, the final piece is packing! Before you start throwing items in a suitcase, take a moment to sit down and write out a packing list, not only for your cosplay but for other items you'll need throughout the weekend. If you're attending a multi-day show, you'll probably be wearing more than cosplay, so maybe this is your time to add a special outfit or that cute new graphic t-shirt. My friends group always plans for one fancy night at cons, featuring tuxes, evening dresses, bowties, and glittering

shoes. And don't forget to throw a swimsuit on the list, especially if the location has a pool.

Once you have your items piling up in a suitcase, make sure you double-check every piece you'll need for your cosplay, as you don't want to miss anything that might be sitting on your ironing board. One option is to pre-pack what you can in a garment or reusable storage bag, so it's protected and easy to fit into your suitcase. For fragile items, take the extra time to securely pack them, or plan to hand-carry. And with the more delicate wigs, you'll want to travel with them styled on the foam head and protected within a cardboard box. It may seem like extra work, but after all the time you have spent on this cosplay, you'll want it to arrive safe and without any issues to fix.

With all of that in mind, here are a few tips for convention planning and packing:

BUILD A COSTUME REPAIR KIT.

Be sure to include thread, needles, scissors, super glue, safety pins, and any additional items you may need to repair your costume in case something happens. And it's likely a con roomie may also put your supplies to use!

DECIDE IF YOU NEED A HANDLER WHILE IN COSPLAY.

Even a basic super suit has its struggles, so aim to have a trusty friend or partner around to help you while in cosplay. Especially for those larger costumes, you will certainly need an assist for doors, stairs, and bathroom breaks.

IRON AND THEN HANG UP YOUR COSPLAY.

Once you arrive at the hotel, take the time to unpack and check each piece of your costume. And when you have a moment, plug in the iron, and press out any wrinkles or lines that have appeared while traveling. A pass of the iron will totally make the difference in that final photo!

A few items in my repair kit include thread and needle, scissors, safety pins, and glue.

138

HAVE WATER AND SNACKS.

It's always good to have snacks on hand for when you're getting into costume, and then to carry with you once you hit the convention floor. Make sure to take breaks to drink water and eat, as you'll be surprised at how fast a day can go by, and you realize you never had a meal.

PACE YOURSELF!

Prepare for a long day on your feet. Make sure to take breaks, or even change into more comfortable shoes. Most convention halls are just a thin carpet over cement flooring, which is fairly unforgiving to most people's feet. And if you're only there for the day, pack a change of clothes for when you're ready to get out of costume.

FOLLOW COSPLAY ETIQUETTE.

Every convention has its own event rules, including for costume and props, so before arriving confirm you'll be able to follow them, along with the unwritten convention code. These can include only bringing harmless props, where you can stop for photos, cosplay consent (see page 142), practicing basic hygiene, and generally being considerate to fellow cosplayers and con staff. And remember to be accommodating when asking a fellow cosplayer for a photo.

FINALLY, MAKE SAFE AND SMART DECISIONS!

Now with your costume packed and logistics locked in, it's time to head to the convention!

A handful of the convention badges I've collected over the last 20 years.

Blending fabric, 3D prints, and foam, CosplayDad_UK poses at MCM London Comic Con in 2022.

Most New Yorkers know it's Comic Con weekend when you're riding the subway next to a Deadpool.

★ ★ MEETING COSPLAYERS AT CONVENTIONS ★ ★

GETTING TO SEE AND MEET COSPLAYERS IS AN EXCIT-ing part of the con experience, but there are some rules and etiquette that you should remember so that everyone is treated with respect. Remember, we're all there to have fun—just because someone is in costume does not explicitly give anyone else permission to touch or say anything inappropriate to that cosplayer.

Embraced officially by New York Comic Con in 2014, and then followed by many conventions around the world, it's now become normal to see *Cosplay Is Not Consent* signs around a convention floor. The phrase shines a light on the inappropriate behavior and sexual harassment experienced by cosplayers at conventions and events. It also serves to remind fans that cosplayers are humans, too. So, when meeting a cosplayer, remember and follow these steps:

1. Respect a person's right to say no to a photo.
2. Keep your hands to yourself.
3. Be kind to one another.

Andy Park, Director of Visual Development, Marvel Studios, signs a poster for a Captain Marvel cosplayer at Comic-Con in 2023.

142

★ ★ WHAT TO DO AT A CONVENTION IN COSPLAY ★ ★

AS MENTIONED EARLIER IN THE BOOK, COSPLAY AND conventions have become synchronous, with each going hand in hand. Throughout a show, there are different events happening across multiple days, from morning to evening, with many things to do in cosplay.

First, you can plan to walk the floor in your new costume. The easiest way to meet fellow fans, learn about con events, and even ask to have your photo taken is by just taking a wander outside of your hotel room. At most conventions, the praise starts the minute you step into an elevator. It is likely, no matter what costume you're wearing, that someone will recognize you and ask you for a photo. It is certainly up to you if you want to be photographed, or even pose with a requestor. There is no expectation for you to say yes, and most people will respect your wishes. Remember, *cosplay is not consent.* That said, if the answer is a heck yes, get ready to strike a pose or two.

While in costume, you'll also run into a few excited fans, ranging from children to adults. Most will move on after grabbing your photo, but some may want to take a moment to chat with you. It could be a question on how you made your costume or prop, or just to share their passion for the character you're cosplaying. It may seem a little strange at first, but it's just another unique convention experience, and honestly, the most heartwarming. There is no need necessarily to get fully into character, but when interacting with children it's nice to lean into your character a little bit, as you might make their day with a moment of magic.

One of the scheduled events that happen at conventions are the cosplay meetups. Usually organized by fellow attendees, meetups are primarily an opportunity for you to meet fellow fans and then join in a series of group photos. They are a great option for first-time cosplayers to debut their costumes, especially as you are guaranteed to have a photo taken, as the *official* photographer for each meetup will usually upload all their photos online later.

Each convention has its iconic locations for meetups; for Dragon Con it's the Hilton back steps, while for Katsucon it's the fabled gazebo. Depending on the size, meetups can get a little hectic, so it's always good to find the organizer and to listen to directions being given. Most are organized via social media, with the date and time posted online in the weeks leading up to the convention. Some conventions even include the meetup schedule on their site or app. And once you're walking the floor, it's likely a fellow cosplayer will come up to you to let you know about the meetup happening later that day.

Outside of the large gatherings, many cosplayers organize smaller, private groups, typically booking a photographer to grab photos. These tend to be calmer affairs and can allow more individual attention from the photographer and fellow cosplayers. Most of these groups form online among a community a few months before a convention, or they may be organized at a previous event.

Although you'll likely run into a few photographers, if you're looking to ensure you get photos of yourself in costume, the best bet is to schedule a photo shoot. Cosplay photography is an art form in and of itself, with a range of styles from photographer to photographer. You could book one who uses the location to add an element to the final image, while others set up with backdrops and lighting to transport you to another world with a little help from Photoshop. This isn't like your senior prom photos; as a photographer myself, I look to collaborate with the cosplayers to create photos we're both excited to share online.

When looking to find and book a photographer, check out fellow cosplayers they've worked with before, or even community groups online, as many

143

(Clockwise from left) Darthpool20bby, Ms.captain.marvel, and Real_yin_cosplay pose for a photo at WonderCon.

will post about their availability for upcoming conventions. And even though your phone can take a great photo, having a professional image of your finished cosplay is always a nice thing to share on your social media and with friends and family.

If you're looking to be more adventurous, almost all conventions have an option for a friendly competition. Typically, the cosplay competition is one of the main events of the weekend. Judged by a panel of fellow cosplayers, industry professionals, and even celebrities, you'll be scored on craftsmanship, accuracy, presentation, and audience reaction. For most cosplayers, the competition is a great way to showcase a new costume in front of a large audience, while also competing for prizes, which can include trophies, money, or even an international trip.

Competitions are broken up into a few different types, with the two primarily focusing on the skill/craft or a planned skit. For those highlighting the craftsmanship, there may be a pre-judging requirement, where you meet with the judges to discuss the process of making the costume before walking on stage. With a masquerade, you'll need to perform a skit pre-choreographed featuring lip synch, dance, or recreation of a scene. Made famous by anime conventions in the 2000s, the masquerade can be *the* event to attend during the weekend. My earliest memories of attending conventions is seeing my friends compete on stage, with intricate costumes and set dressings, sometimes even winning best in show.

Not all competitions require you to walk on a stage in front of thousands of people. Some conventions

have hall costume contests, where you can enter the same day and have your costume judged quietly in a private room. This could be a good option if you're not ready to strut down a stage's runway just yet.

If you're interested in competing at your next convention, check out the con's site early, as many do require you to enter online, with some having a limited number of contestants allowed. And don't fret if you don't win that first time, as there will always be a next time. Remember, cosplay is about having fun, with the added value of showing off some skill.

Besides meetups and competitions, there are so many other things to do in costume, with one being to meet the creator who designed the character, or even the actor who brought them to life on screen. From artist alley to a panel or an autograph session, there are countless ways to show off your cosplay. Many comic creators talk about their joy in seeing their designs becoming real through cosplay. And your photo moment with that famous actor can be even more special when you approach them dressed in a costume.

Organized online before the convention, these Silver Age cosplayers agreed to build their specific characters to debut at WonderCon.

★ ★ WHICH CONVENTIONS TO ATTEND ★ ★

*WITH THE SHEER NUMBER OF CONVENTIONS HAPPEN-*ing every weekend, there are likely many options near or far to add to your list. When deciding on a convention, you'll want to ask yourself a few questions to decide which ones work best for you.

First, do you have friends or a community attending? If so, it's easy enough to add that show to the list, knowing you'll have a support group for when in costume and people to make plans with throughout the day. Or is there a creator or celebrity on the guest list

you'd like to meet? We have all gone to a convention because of a guest. I once flew to a show in Chicago for forty-eight hours to get my photo with Brie Larson. Maybe you're looking to book a photo shoot and know a convention has incredible locations that match your cosplay. Katsucon has become one of the must-visit East Coast conventions because of the Gaylord Hotel's white marble esthetic.

Are you looking for a smaller, local show that is close enough for a day trip, or do you have a little more budget and want to finally attend that famous convention across the country? The size of the show will determine what fandoms will be highlighted. Smaller shows will typically spotlight one genre, such as just comics or tabletop gaming, while larger conventions have the staff, schedule, and space to celebrate multiple genres.

Each convention is special in its own unique way, and you'll discover which ones are a must each year, or once every few years. After attending more than a hundred conventions, I've compiled a list of some of my favorites, especially for cosplayers.

THE MAJOR SHOWS

- Anime Expo in Los Angeles
- Dragon Con in Atlanta
- Fantasy Basel in Basel, Switzerland
- MCM London Comic Con

- MegaCon in Orlando
- New York Comic Con
- San Diego Comic-Con

COMIC CREATOR HEAVY SHOWS

- C2E2 in Chicago
- Emerald City Comic Con in Seattle

- HeroesCon in Charlotte
- WonderCon in Anaheim

VIDEO GAME CONVENTIONS

- DreamHack in Jönköping, Sweden
- Gamescom in Cologne, Germany

- PAX East in Boston and West in Seattle

ANIME AND MANGA CONVENTIONS

- A-Kon in Dallas
- AnimeCentral in Chicago
- Japan Expo in Paris, France

- Katsucon in Washington, DC
- Sakura-Con in Seattle

★ ★ MEETUPS OUTSIDE OF CONVENTIONS ★ ★

IF YOU STILL WANT TO CAPTURE A NICE PHOTO OF your cosplay, but wading through large groups of people at a convention is not your thing or even in your budget, there is the option to attend a non-convention gathering or even schedule a local, private shoot with a cosplay photographer.

As the cosplay community has grown, it was inevitable that we'd want to get together more than a couple times a year. Especially with the advancement of digital cameras and gear, it became more accessible for photographers to organize non-con events with cosplayers. Unlike conventions, these gatherings are typically not advertised online and consist of just a series of photo shoots. But what they do allow is access to locations, interiors, and sets that are not the standard at conventions. In the past, I've attended one event at an urban, almost-abandoned factory. And I know of friends in Europe who have booked a

Using found locations in London, photographer Carlos Adama transports these Loki cosplayers to the TVA.

147

castle for a gathering. These occasions allow you to meet new cosplayers and photographers, while also granting more time to get the perfect shot with that golden light.

And if you're looking for that wholly individual attention with a photographer, then the best plan is to book your own photo shoot. Most cosplay photographers are certainly willing to meet up outside of a convention, especially if they are a fan of your cosplay. Reach out to your local photographer to decide on a place (making sure you check that you can photograph there), date, and time, and get ready to spend the day posing.

Captured at C2E2 with help from additional light sources, photographer Chris Gallevo recreated the Hawkeye poster with cosplayers Katrinavera and Minjaassassin.

Photographer Food and Cosplay used an actual arcade to shoot this epic photo of Shirak's Jubilee cosplay.

★ ★ PHOTOGRAPHER AND COSPLAYER TIPS FOR PHOTO SHOOTS ★ ★

COSPLAY PHOTOGRAPHY HAS CERTAINLY EVOLVED since Nobuyuki Takahashi first coined the term. With the introduction of digital photography, cell phones, and LED lights, the possibilities are endless for the final product you can achieve. As I cut my teeth at conventions with a camera in my hand, here are some tips for preparing for a photo shoot that either a cosplayer or photographer can follow.

SCHEDULING A PHOTO SHOOT

The easiest way to schedule a photo shoot is to reach out via social media. Both cosplayers and photographers will post their availability online, but you also don't have to wait. As a convention or event nears, send along a message about your interest to kick off the conversation.

And if you're not sure where to start, there are online groups, including on Facebook, that help connect photographers and cosplayers for photo shoots. Once you're both on board, make sure to confirm date, time, and location.

FINDING A LOCATION

Every convention has a multitude of options for backdrops, from classical white marble to a gritty, dark parking garage. Before you meet for a shoot, check out the different areas that would work best for your costume. This is true for both cosplayers and photographers. I always appreciate a tip from a cosplayer for a new location I didn't know of before.

Outside of conventions, photo studios are an option for a more controlled set, but typically require additional budget for rental and equipment. With cost in mind, outdoor locations are the usual preference for cosplayers. I have taken many photos at local parks, and sometimes a graffiti wall is fun to play with. Before deciding on a location, make sure you

do not need to get permission or approval to use any private property.

PRE-PREP FOR THE PHOTO SHOOT

This is more for a photographer, but you never want to pack your camera bag the morning of a photo shoot and realize your batteries aren't charged. Leading up to the date, double-check your gear, rent any

Ashanyxx's partner grabs a quick photo on her phone during a photoshoot with Si.Kutzer.

Photographer Pat Loika demonstrates how a little post-production helps Bishopcosplay jump off the page.

additional lenses you may want, empty your memory cards, and yes, charge those batteries.

For cosplayers, get your costume ready before the day of the shoot. Make any touch-ups needed, secure any loose parts, and comb out your wig. This will ensure a smooth morning as you prepare to walk out the door.

COME PREPARED WITH IDEAS

We all have expectations of the finished photos, so take some time to rough out some ideas, either on paper or by saving references. The photographer may not always know all the source material, so it can be helpful to come prepared to walk them through your character and the world they exist in.

HAVE AN ASSISTANT OR HANDLER ON SET

It never hurts to have an extra hand or two to assist with a costume or hold a reflector. And by having more people nearby, they'll be able to keep an eye on

costume fixes or just watch the phones and bags, plus even grab a few behind-the-scenes moments for your social media later!

KEEP AN EYE ON THE LITTLE THINGS

With costume and wigs, there is always that one piece that doesn't want to behave, so for photographers, it's important to keep an eye on the whole picture. Are there a few wig flyaways, or did the belt begin to ride up as the cosplayer posed? Catching these things before you take the photos will help limit any tedious post-production edits and make sure everyone feels happy about the final product.

COMMUNICATE THROUGHOUT THE PROCESS

From booking to day of and after, it's important to keep communication open. Be honest about what each of you are looking to capture, including any edits you'll want to make. And if you're running late,

150

be considerate and keep everyone informed. We've all had that hiccup when getting into a costume, or a photo shoot running behind. Being forthcoming will help keep all the emotions on level ground.

It's easy for anticipation to grow while waiting for the final images, but don't pressure the photographer to edit photos faster than agreed. Everyone has a different timeline in how they process photos. But then also don't leave a cosplayer waiting for weeks or months.

FINALLY, BE KIND AND TAG!

For most this is just a hobby, so everyone is giving a bit of their time, from making a costume to editing a photo, and it's considerate and almost expected to tag on social media.

Celebration of Marvel Cosplay Covers

★ ★ ★

Lost to time and those long boxes in your parents' basement, there have been a few Marvel comics graced with people in costumes throughout the years. One of the classics is the cover of *Spider-Woman #50*, from 1983, and one of the most expensive covers of the time. Unlike the future Marvel cosplay variants, the eleven people on the cover weren't necessarily just fans, but all Marvel employees or their spouses. Composed from several photos taken by fellow bull-pen member Elliot Brown (who would become the *unofficial* photographer during his decade in the office), it's a great reflection of the crazy and *anything goes* atmosphere of 1980s Marvel.

Now let's flash forward more than thirty years later to 2015, when the idea of doing a series of variants featuring cosplayers was pitched at a creative retreat by Brian Michael Bendis. From there, the proposal would end up on my desk, with the question: *Can we make this happen?* And the answer was obviously a resounding *yes*.

Captured from New York City to Atlanta, at conventions and on location, the twenty-one cosplayers highlighted just a piece of the diverse cosplay community. It was such a success that an additional fourteen variants were released the following year. For each cosplayer, many of whom had been fans since childhood, the experience of being on an actual cover was a dream come true.

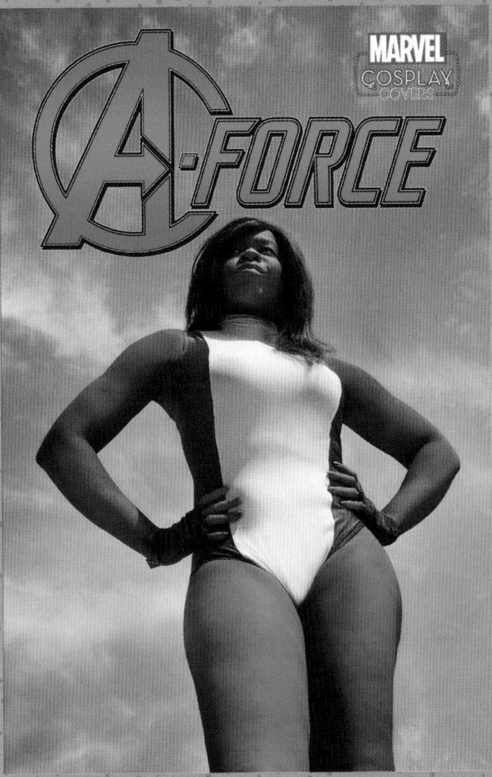
MARVEL
COSPLAY
COVERS
A-FORCE

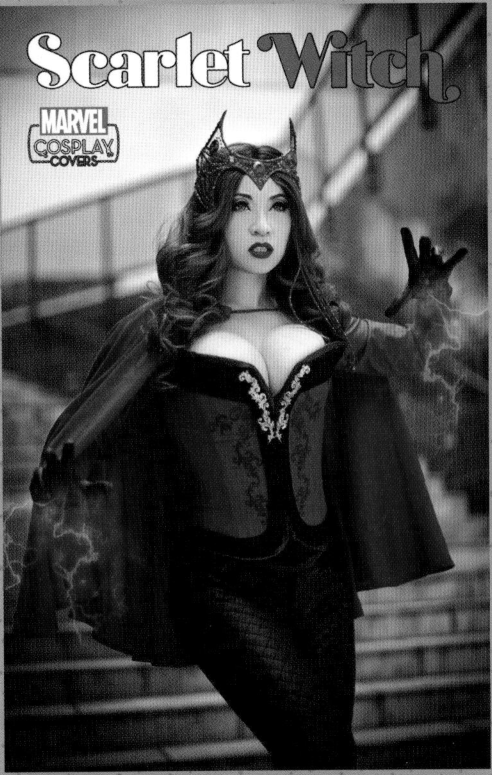
Scarlet Witch
MARVEL
COSPLAY
COVERS

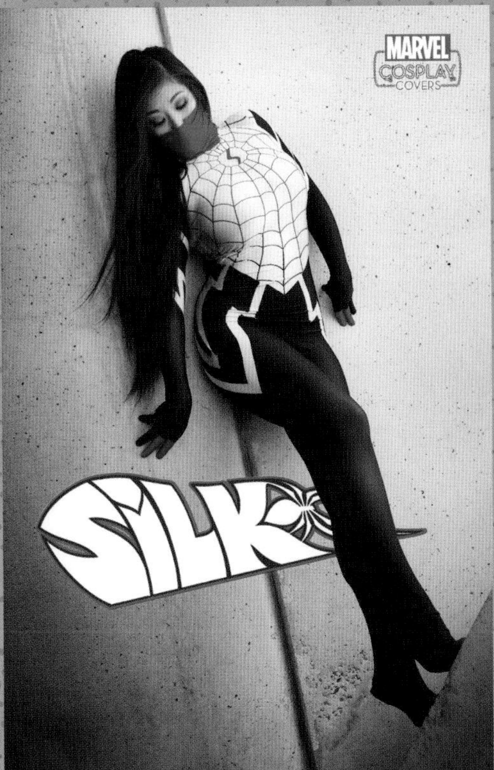
MARVEL
COSPLAY
COVERS
SILK

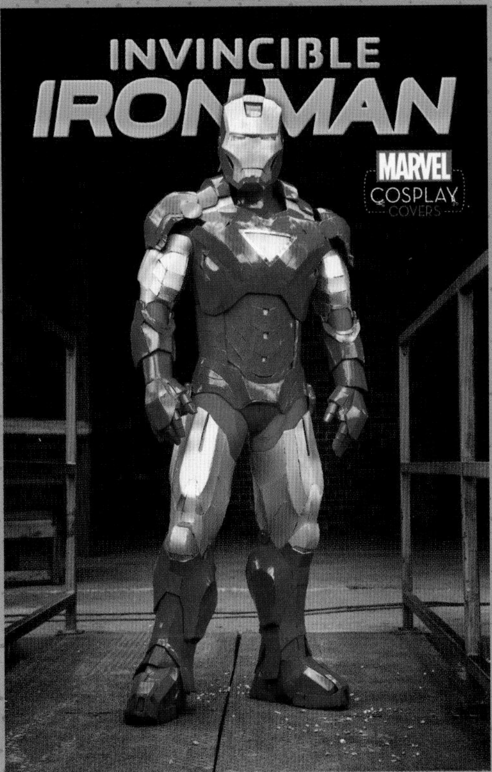
INVINCIBLE
IRON MAN
MARVEL
COSPLAY
COVERS

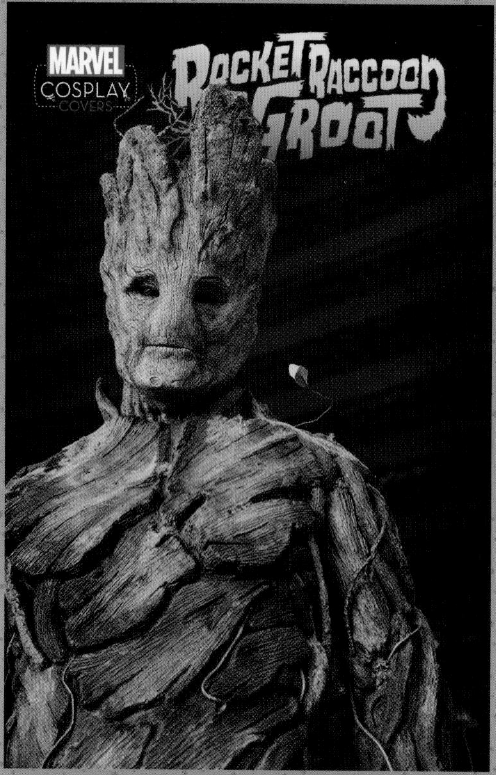
MARVEL
COSPLAY
COVERS
ROCKET RACCOON
GROOT
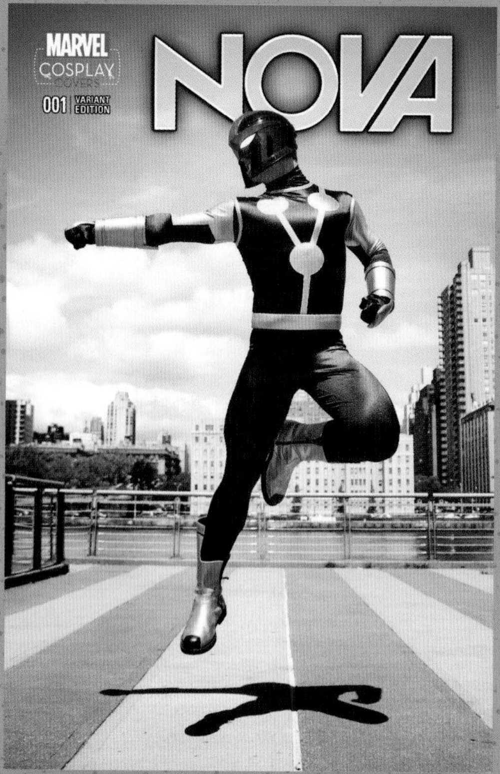
MARVEL
COSPLAY
COVERS
001 VARIANT EDITION
NOVA
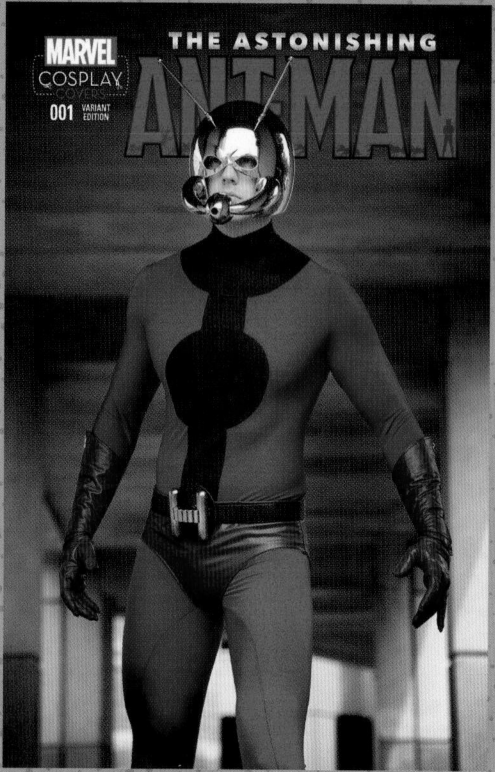
MARVEL
COSPLAY
COVERS
001 VARIANT EDITION
THE ASTONISHING
ANT-MAN
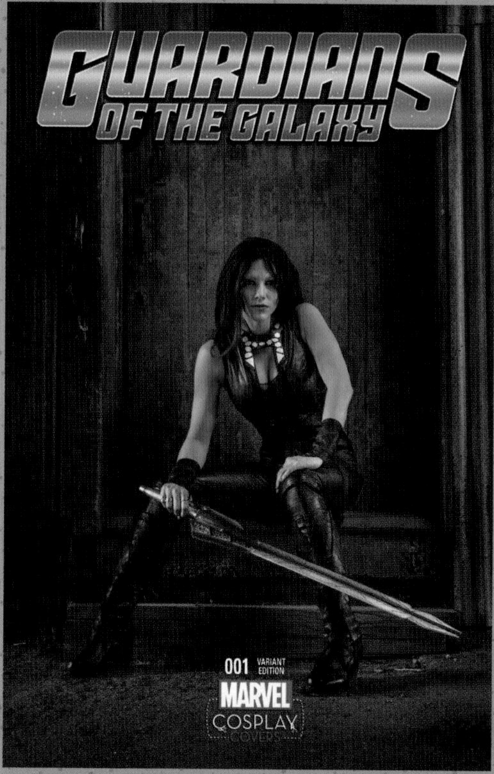
GUARDIANS OF THE GALAXY
001 VARIANT EDITION
MARVEL
COSPLAY
COVERS

★ ★ THE SOCIAL MEDIA GAME ★ ★

YOU'VE LIKELY DISCOVERED COSPLAY THANKS TO social media. Just like conventions and cosplay, now social media and cosplay go hand in hand. That isn't to say you *have* to post your cosplay online, but we wouldn't be here as a community without those early forums that grew into Facebook and now Instagram and TikTok.

No matter if you have a small or large following, I highly recommend you post and share your work. We cosplayers love to see images and videos of builds along with the final photos. Each post inspires us, maybe even giving us the motivation to start a new costume or even finish the one sitting half-done in the closet. For many of the cosplayers I've worked with throughout the years at Marvel, I initially discovered them via an online search.

A post can easily connect you to new friends and even a specialized community. Over the years,

cosplayers have come together to form collaborations to support one another online, especially around marginalized groups. From the Replica Prop Forum to Kamui's Cosplay Community on Facebook and now the SheProp! Community on Instagram, each has helped support, teach, and highlight cosplayers through the years.

And like many creators and influencers online, there is the possibility for cosplayers to also build a brand online and turn it into a career. That is a road many cosplayers have paved, with Yaya Han leading the way. But it isn't for everyone, so if that is something you're interested in, it's best to learn from what they've done while forging your own path.

As much as we'd like to ignore the other side of the internet, posting an image of yourself, especially in costume, can open you up to both positive and negative comments. For some reason, complete

The She-Prop! community meet-up at Emerald City Comic Con.

155

internet strangers feel the need to leave purposely hurtful comments on a photo or video. And it certainly does suck. But it is up to us as a community to come together to support one another and continue to ensure that cosplay can be a safe and supportive space for everyone. So keep using the tools of social media: post, tag, share, and block.

★ ★ PACKING IT AWAY UNTIL THE NEXT TIME ★ ★

FINALLY, AFTER THE ADVENTURE OF BUILDING YOUR first cosplay, debuting it at a convention, and then sharing it online, it's time to return home to recover, before packing it away until the next event. Before you stuff the pieces into a box and shove it to the back of a closet, I'd like to pass along a few tips that should help preserve it until you'd like to wear it again.

As you unpack your suitcase, keep all the elements of your cosplay organized together. Fabric pieces and smaller foam elements can be stored in resealable bags. Just like your patterns, on the outside of the bag, label what the costume is and what's inside. Depending on the size of the costume, you might be able to fit it all into one larger bag, or maybe it's spread out through a few. And for items that are too large to fold or roll, such as Loki's coat, you may want to preserve it in a hanging garment bag.

Next, for those delicate foam and 3D pieces, safely wrap each item, using packaging material or scrap fabric, supporting any curves as you pack them. One thing to note is limiting contact between painted objects and your fabric elements, as paint may rub off over time. And with wigs, those styled may need to be left on the foam head, while others can be tucked into their original packaging or a similar bag or box, after giving them a brush to get rid of any knots or snarls.

For storing, there are a wide variety of options of storage containers, especially if you have the space in a basement or garage. But for those with limited closet space, like my New York apartment, a good option is to use your suitcases for storage. And as you begin to build more and more costumes, make sure to label any boxes, especially for when you go to look for that one wig from four years ago.

Then there are the items you're proud to show off, such as your first sword prop or a hand-embroidered

Cosplayers pose at the first-ever Hellfire Gala at San Diego Comic-Con in 2023.

156

TOP: Michael and Lety Garcia as Nova and Captain Marvel at a red carpet event.

RIGHT: Ødfel poses in her lace-front Captain Britain wig at Katsucon.

jacket. In my office, I always have a costume displayed on my dress form and props displayed on a few shelves. It's proven a good background for video calls, while a reminder of something I should be proud of. A kind of trophy! And maybe it's even a suggestion to start that next project. Because once you've discovered cosplay, it's kind of hard to stop. We all have that next project already in our minds, with image references saved, possibly fabric already in a cart, so it's never too soon to get started!

I've been incredibly lucky to meet so many friends through cosplay.

★ ★ ★ Conclusion ★ ★ ★

★ ★ THIS IS NOT THE END, BUT JUST THE START! ★ ★

There is a human desire in all of us to want to feel like we belong; we all are looking to find a community in which to feel loved and treasured. Like many of us, I spent most of my earlier years struggling to find that feeling. But it was through this magical hobby that I found this home, a place to build a career and friendships around the world, which all led to writing this book.

OVER THE YEARS AT MARVEL, I REALIZED I HAD a unique opportunity to build a platform for cosplay. Starting with those early forum posts, to pitching new events online and then videos, I was always looking for a way to add some element of cosplay into what we were doing on Marvel.com. At conventions, it became natural for cosplayers to flock to the booth, either for a stage event or just to show off their costumes. For Dragon Con, fans put up with signing countless releases year after year to be a part of the site's photo gallery from the giant gathering. And for years I pitched having cosplayers at a film's premiere, to the point where they are almost the best part of a red carpet. With every high, there was of course a low, but along the way I knew I had an incredible community of friends standing behind me.

Which is what allowed me to write this book. I couldn't have done this without Raisa, Mark, Indra, Kisa, Marc, and Tony. These pages are the true story of cosplay—a mixture of friends, new and old, coming together to build something great, alongside the countless others who helped, sending photos, sharing memories, and just being our sanity checks.

As I wrap up, I will say my goal was to teach you a new skill and inspire you to finally start that dream Marvel cosplay. I've already started pulling out patterns for my next Captain Marvel project. So, whether you're a seasoned cosplayer or brand-new to the hobby, I hope you've enjoyed this wild ride, learning about this community and the techniques to make your own costume. I can't wait to see your brand-new cosplays out in the world. Welcome to the magical world of cosplay!

Marvel Cosplay Around the World

★ ★ ★

From sea to sea, country to country, convention to convention, cosplayers have celebrated their passion for Marvel and its characters. I'd love to share just a few of the cosplayers from around the world.

LEFT TO RIGHT: (Left) Cosplay in Japan has expanded past anime and manga, as Ken Edge as Iron Man and (Middle) Hiragi as Deadpool demonstrate. (Right) Showcasing a wide variety of crafting skills are JJ_mkmr as Sylvie and Villainsprince as Loki, captured by Osa_gekka, also from Japan.

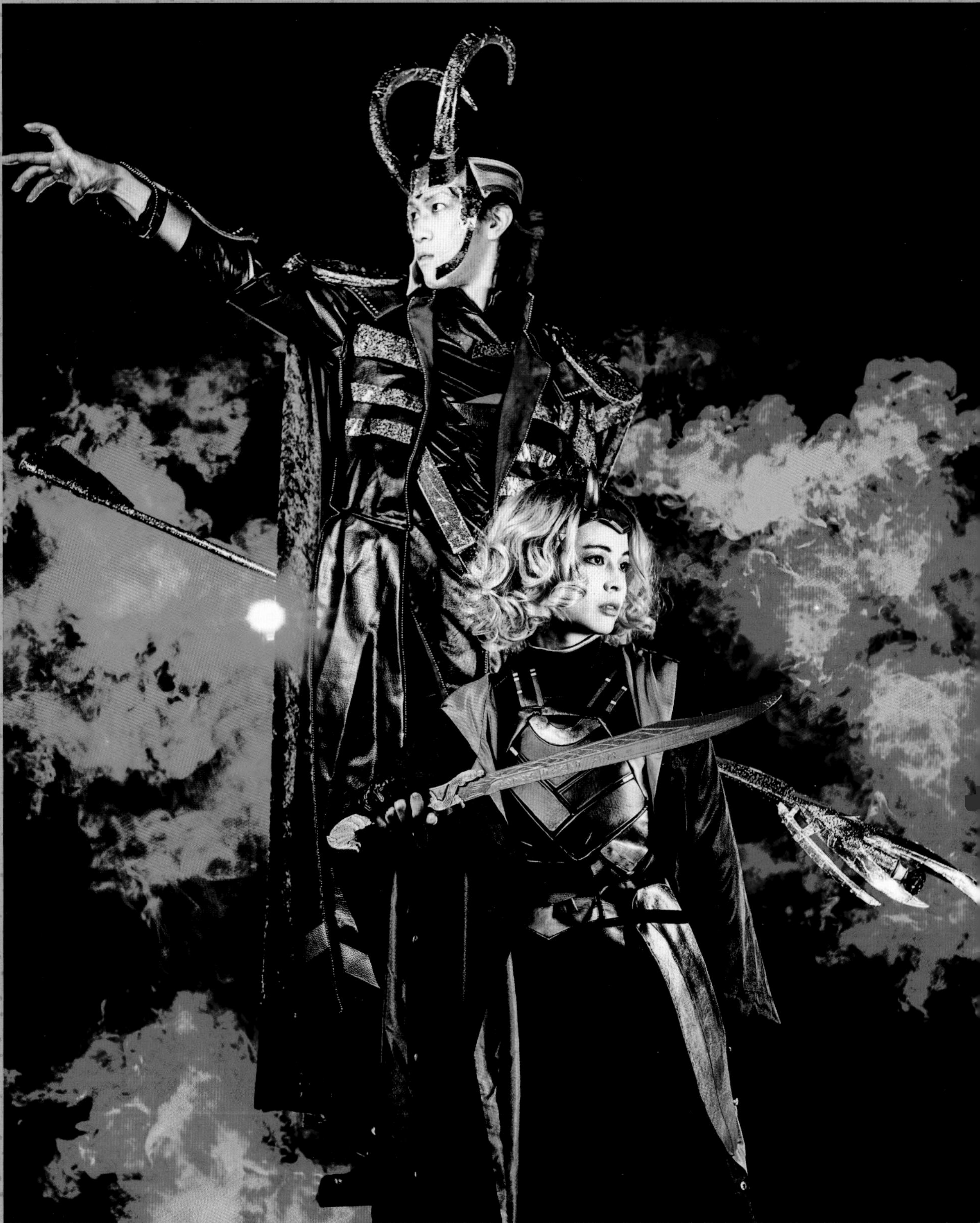

ABOVE: Straight from the comic to a costume, Captain_Britt brings the new Elektra Daredevil to life for WonderCon 2023.
TOP RIGHT: The Loki love certainly transcends countries as Mar.K poses at a local convention in Japan.
BOTTOM RIGHT: From all the way across the Pacific in New Zealand, Sanit Klamchanuan brings his version of Nova to life.

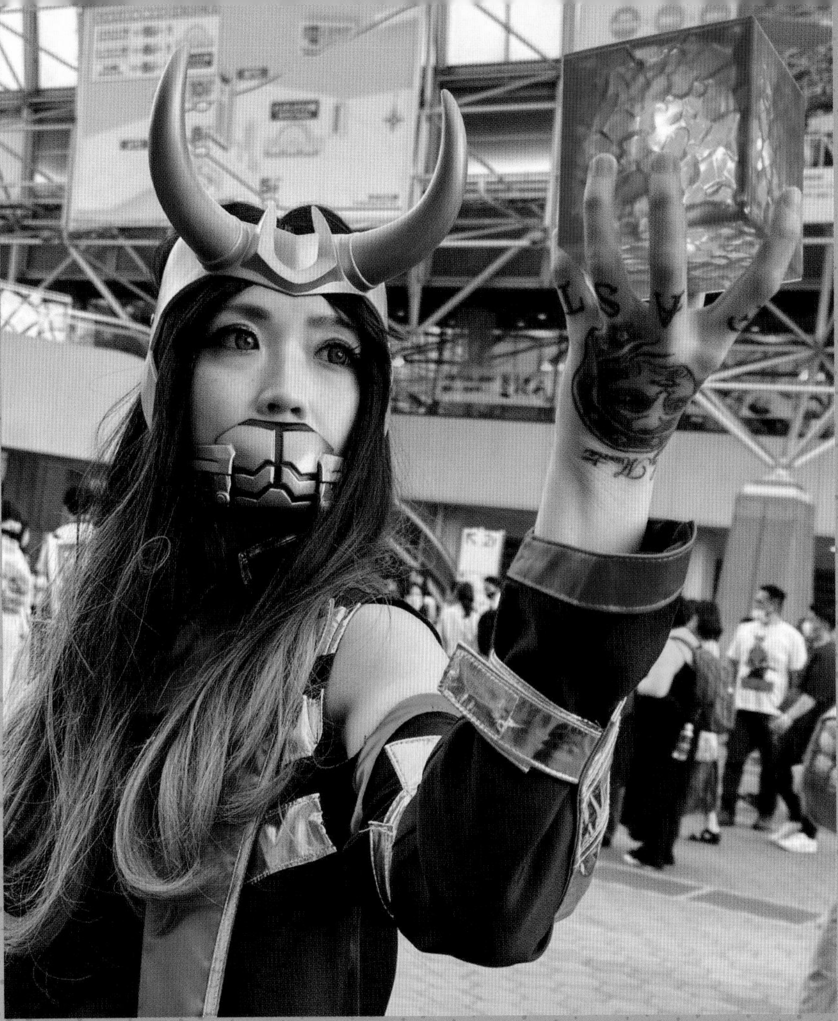

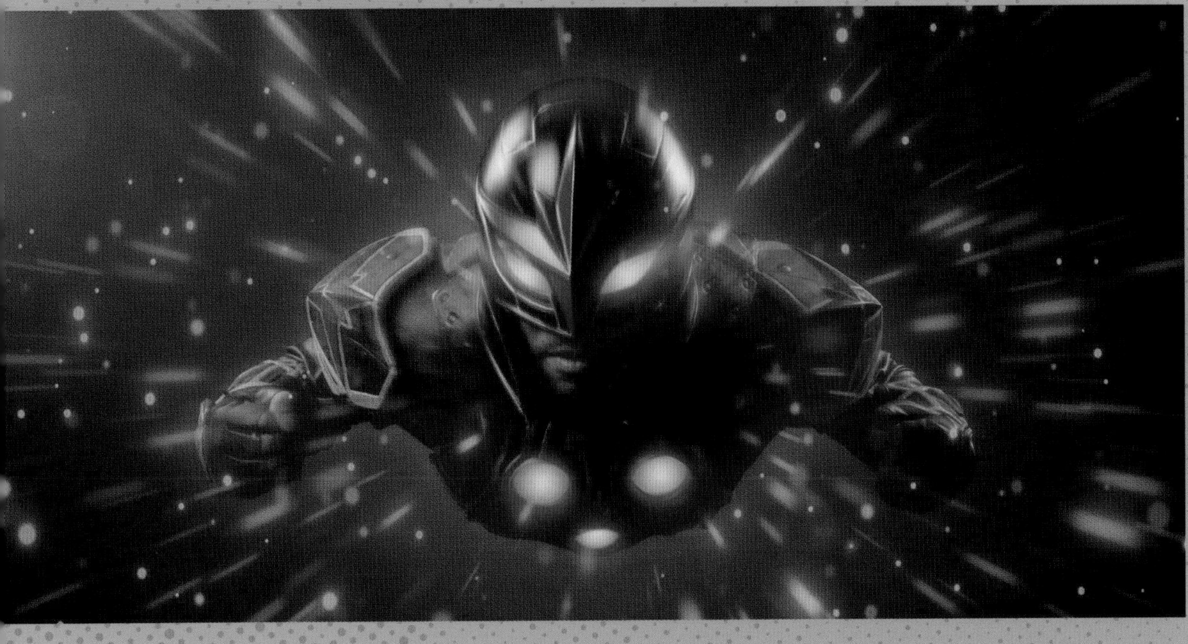

LEFT TO RIGHT: (Left) In South America, Constanza represents Chile in her America Chavez cosplay. (Middle) The 2023 Indian Cosplay Champion, Medha Srivastava, is ready to protect the Black Panther in her Dora Milaje cosplay. (Right) Helalipop brings a new look to Ghost Rider at New York Comic Con in 2018.

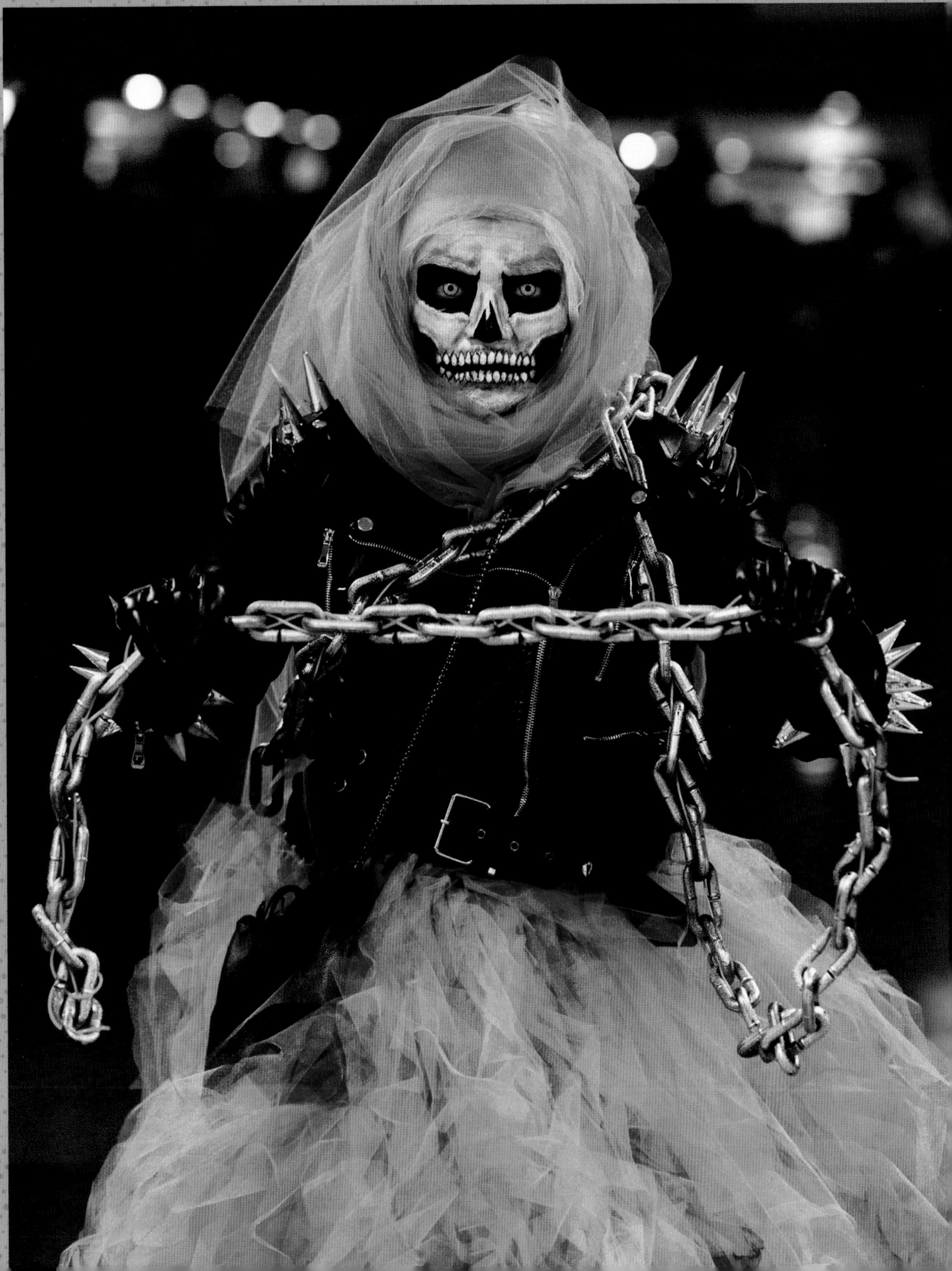

ACKNOWLEDGMENTS

THIS BOOK WOULD NOT HAVE BEEN POSSIBLE WITHOUT the following incredible human beings. My editor, Britny Perilli, was my best cheerleader through every step of this process and pushed me to be the writer I didn't realize I could be. Everyone at Running Press, from the editing team to design to marketing—thank you for supporting this book and the cosplay community.

The Marvel team, whom I had the honor to work with for many years and who then encouraged me to actually write a book. This book wouldn't be here without Sven Larsen, Jeremy West, Jeff Youngquist, and Sarah Singer, let alone the many, many great people who assisted me in building a cosplay community at Marvel. There are truly too many names to list here, but I want to thank John Cerilli, Ryan Penagos, Adri Cowan, Jason Latorre, and Nicole Ciaramella.

As I've said countless times, I and this book wouldn't be here without every cosplayer, photographer, and friend I've met along this magical ride. Thank you to every person who attended an event at a convention, agreed to be a part of one of my projects, answered my countless messages online, and entrusted me with your photos and cosplay. I am so lucky to be able to have so many friends around the world, especially my always incredible chaos friends group in New York City.

Lastly, to my parents, a mathematician and a scientist, who have supported their artistic and creative-minded daughter in every adventure I've set myself on, from purchasing me my first camera at fifteen to helping me move to New York for college and then trusting me that this Marvel job might be a good place to hang out for a while. Throughout it all, my greatest accomplishment is to just make them proud. Love you, Mom and Dad.

★ ★ ★ ★ ★ ★

Courtesy of Judy Stephens: XII, 3, 1 (bottom), 10 (bottom), 13 (bottom), 17, 20, 22, 24, 25, 32, 34, 35, 36 (bottom), 125, 132, 138, 139, 142, 158

Courtesy of Marvel: XV (left), 11, 14 (bottom), 36 (top), 37, 39, 40, 50, 51, 62, 63, 64, 68, 76, 77, 78, 83, 90, 91, 92, 97, 106, 107, 108, 109, 111, 127, 152, 153, 154

Alan Lavery: 82, 89

Alexandra Lee Studios: 80

AliMalik: 165

Alyssa_the_coco: 157

Bill Watters: 5

Brett Downen: 26, 30

Cameko Cosplay: 33

Carlos Adama: XV (right), 147, 176

Chris Gallevo: 128, 148 (right)

Constanza: 164 (left)

Darien Hester: 121

Dave Lucchesi: 123

Dax Exclamationpoint: 129

Food and Cosplay: 148 (left)

Giant Robot John: 124

Hiragi / pigpool_dead: 160 (right)

Howie Mizuka: 145

Indra Rojas: 65, 66, 70, 71, 72, 73, 74, 75

Jasmine La Sha: 144

Jason Laboy: VI, 151 (bottom)

Jay Tablante, Ara Fernando, Javey Villones, Raffy Tesoro, and Ryder Aquino: 10 (top)

Jeff Duhon: 8

Jeremy Wallace: 18

Josh Shot Photo: 155

Kathrine Zan: IX, X (left), XIV, XII (bottom), XIV, 12

Katie O'Neill: 139

Ken__edgecap: 160 (left)

Kisa Watton: 84, 85, 86, 87, 88

Littlenoisephoto: 163 (bottom)

Madison May: 94

Mar.K: 163 (top)

Marc Schwerin: 93, 96, 99, 100, 101, 102, 103, 104

Mark Matthews: 52, 54, 57, 58, 59, 60, 61

Matthew Chiang: 133

Mike Tuffley: 134

MineralBlu: 157

Nicole Ciaramella: X (right), 4, 6, 13 (top), 14 (top)

Osa_gekka: 161

Pat Loika: XI, 112, 150, 156, 159 , 168 (featuring cosplayer Amanda Lynne Shafer)

Patrick Sun: 135

Raisa Karim: 31, 41, 42, 44, 46, 47, 48, 49

Rem Ritrato: 136

Ron Gejon: 16, 126, 151 (top)

Si.Kutzer: 149

So Say We All Photography: 79

Tony Ray: 110, 115, 116, 117, 119, 120

Vic Treviño: 105

World Of Gwendana: 162

Yash Indap: 164 (right)

A very special thanks to all our Marvel Becoming cosplayers: 2PlayerGame; A2 Cosplay; Aaron Rivin; Alicia Marie; Allen Hansard; Alys Adamantium; Amanda Lynn Shafer; Amberskies; Ashlynne Dae; Ben Alcaraz, Silvia Vargas, and family; Beverly Downen; Binkxy; Black Zero Cosplay; Blerd Vision; Blikku; Brett Yee; Cap Santiago; Charles Xavier; Chris Burns; Colana Suzuki; CutiePieSensei; Dale Oliver; Daniel Petruccio; Danielle Kane; David McKahan; DJ Spider; Eddie Pagan; God Saves the Queens Fashions; Hannah Kent; Hendoart; Hex Mortis; HurleyFx; Indra Rojas; Irene Yu; Jasmin

Loves You; Jax Cosplay; Jes Reaves; Jess Jupiter; Jessica Dru Johnson; Jinglebooboo; Johnny Junkers; Kearstin; Kit Quinn; Lauren of Castle Corsetry; Lauren of PitchFork Cosplay; Lexi Momo; Lizard Leigh; Maid of Might; Marc Schwerin; Mary Cahela; Maryjaneromanoff; Melly McShane; Michael G.; Michelle Waffle-Otero; Mike Prost; Miracole Burns; Miss Mad Love; Miya Tamlyn; Realtdragon; Rose Romanova; Ryan Green; Sharon Rose; Shirley Melendez; Sidney Cumbie; SoloRoboto; Taboo of the Black Eyed Peas; Titan Cosplay; Tyler Smithart; Vanessa Walton; Vickie Bane; and Yaya Han.

And the crafters behind the scenes: Aria Ferraro; CoreGeek; DialC Costumes; Fon Davis and Fonco;

Jesse Thaxton; Keaghlan Ashley; Lindsay Jane; Miya Tamlyn; and SMPdesigns.

Marvel Cosplay Covers featuring: Aaron Rivin; Alana Waffles; Allen Lee Hansard; Amanda Lynne Shafer; Cap Santiago; Contagious Costuming; Corrine Vitek; Crystal Melton; Dale Oliver; DJ Spider; Eddie Newsome; Elena Strikes; HurleyFx; Johnny Junkers; Kalel Sean; Kathrine Zan; Kevin Spooner; Knobel Creations; Lauren Matesic; Michael Cox; Mike Powell; Miss Kit Quinn; Patrick "Rick" Lane; Pierre Demery; Riki "Riddle" Lecotey; Sarah Jean Maefs; ScorpKing Costuming; SoloRoboto Industries; Soni Balestier; Wesley Johnson; Yashuntafun Cosplay; and Yaya Han.

INDEX

Note: Page numbers in italics refer to photos and their captions.

D

V

W

X

Y

Z

ABOUT THE AUTHOR

JUDY STEPHENS IS AN AUTHOR, PRODUCER, AND COS-player with ever-changing rainbow-colored hair. With more than fifteen years at Marvel, Judy has worked in production of news and pop culture–based content, including photos, video, and multimedia, as the company evolved from a small, family-like operation to the worldwide phenomenon it is now.

Since attending her first anime and comic convention in 2004, Judy has traveled the world as staff, photographer, guest, and attendee of more than a hundred conventions, meeting cosplayers from California to New Zealand to Chile. As part of her inclusion in the cosplay community, she is well known as an advocate for cosplay at Marvel and Disney, with contributions including *Marvel Becoming*, Marvel Cosplay Covers, Costoberfest, organizing the Marvel Cosplay Contests, social media coverage, and most recently Marvel's 616-episode *Suit Up* on Disney+. Over the last two decades, she has also cosplayed more than thirty characters, including her well-known Captain Marvel.

A proud Queens resident, where she lives with her two cats, she spends her free time enjoying the city, working out, and traveling with friends. Judy is currently a podcast producer and co-author of the book *Super Visible: The Story of the Women of Marvel*.